JAZZ LICKS

Comprehensive Studies for Flute & C Instruments

by SARPAY ÖZÇAĞATAY

FOREWORD

Jazz licks are among the most common patterns in improvisation-based music. These patterns are very helpful in understanding chord and note relationships, smooth transitions between chords, and are a great way to improve agility on your instrument.

The purpose of this book is to develop a better understanding of how certain tensions are used on different kinds of dominant chords, deduce situations in which certain tension combinations are 'available' over dominant chords, and learn how to apply these tension combinations to create lines and licks. This book will also help you develop your ear by applying these licks to all of the chord variations found throughout the book.

Below are the fundamental methods for creating jazz licks;

1) Using diatonic notes in chord tonality
2) Incorporating non-diatonic notes into chord tonality
3) Chromatic approaches to chord tonality

Please note If you need more information about any of the methods listed above, it is recommended that you take the studies from this book with you to a professional instructor to help connect these concepts.

There are many different jazz cadences in jazz song forms (e.g., II-V7-I, I-VI-II-V7-I, I-IV-I, V7-I, and so on...). In this book, you will study the most common jazz cadence: the II-V7-I chord structure. Each example has 3 variations in all 12 major keys. All examples are written in 4/4.

Note that the patterns may/will contain chromatic note approaches, also known as jazz approaches in different note amounts.

Once you've completed the studies in the main section, there is a bonus section containing examples with uncommon chord progressions in varying time signatures (e.g., 3/4, 7/4, 5/8, 6/8 etc.) for you to try. Here, you are encouraged to reinforce the principles learned in the main section by applying them in different harmonic and time environments.

The articulations in the book are written for the flute *however*, you as the reader are encouraged to adjust these articulations for your convenience. Any readers playing a transposing instrument are encouraged to transpose these licks into your corresponding key.

Thanks so much for investing in this book and I wish you well on your musical journey!

HOW TO CREATE A JAZZ LICK

Tonality is set to: C Major

* 9 & 13 are natural tensions

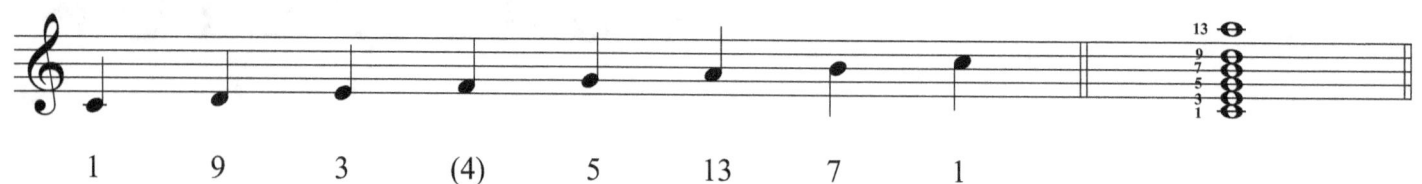

Pattern Source: Cmaj7 chord arpeggio

The arpeggio pattern diatonically implied over the II-V7-I chord progression

Natural Tensions (9) & (13) applied over the arpeggio pattern

Altered Tensions (b9) & (b13) applied over the arpeggio pattern

Using rhythms makes patterns sounding more musical

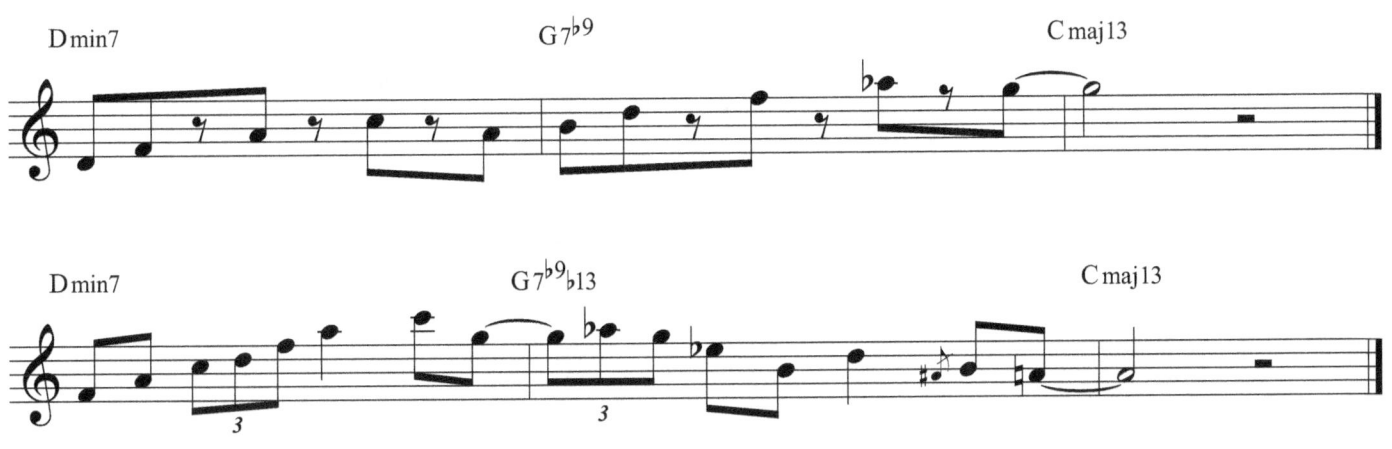

Chromatic Approach Pattern Applied

As you see from all of the examples above, a single diatonic arpeggio pattern can be a useful tool in creating a jazz lick. Note that there are a few more non-diatonic tensions (#9 and #11) that can be applied over the dominant chords as well.

There are also non-diatonic tensions (not listed in this book) that can be applied over minor and major chords. While studying this book, it is recommended that you explore application of tension over other chord qualities.

Also, it is recommended that the reader take a look at some of the other books by the author, Sarpay Özçağatay - specifically UNLOCK Vol. I *The Jazz Flute* and UNLOCK Vol. II *Technical Exercises*. There, you'll find more exercises that can easily be converted into cool sounding jazz licks.

JAZZ LICKS AND TENSION USAGE

C MAJOR

♮9 - ♮13 (Diatonic tensions)

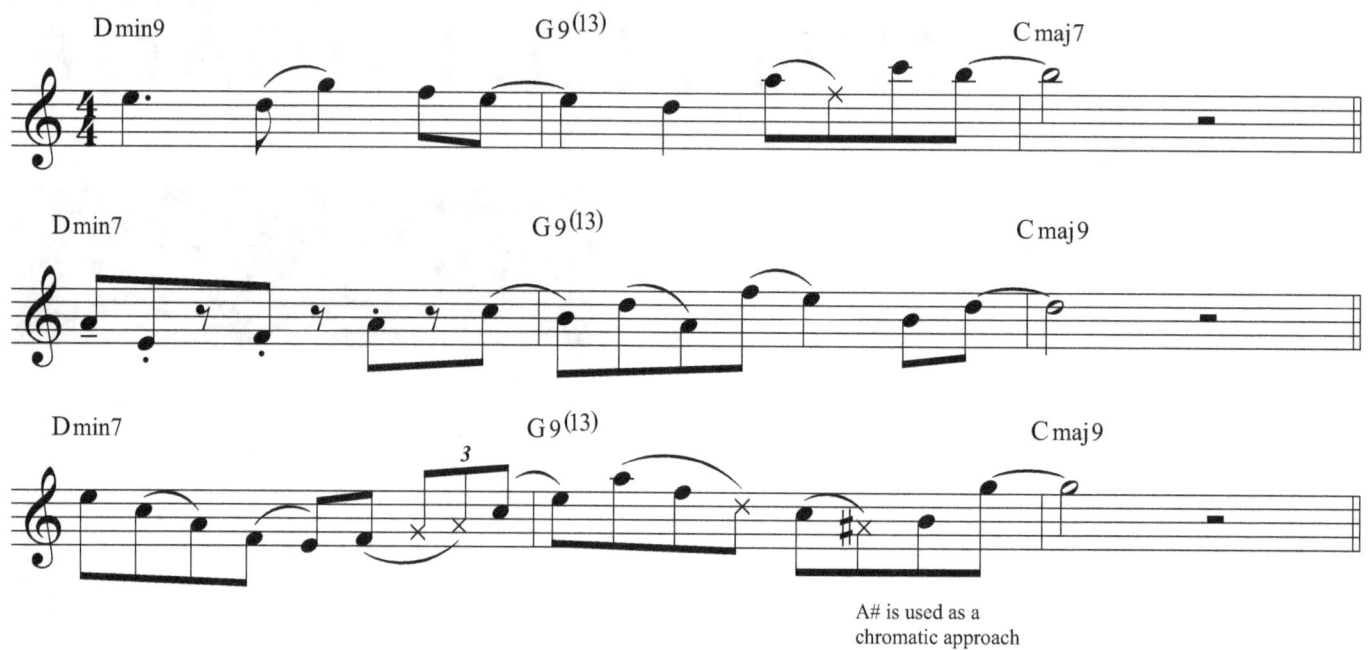

A# is used as a chromatic approach

♭9 - ♮13

the pattern over G7 begins one beat early

X = Ghost Note

♭9 - ♭13

♯9 - ♭13

♮9-#11

♭9-#11

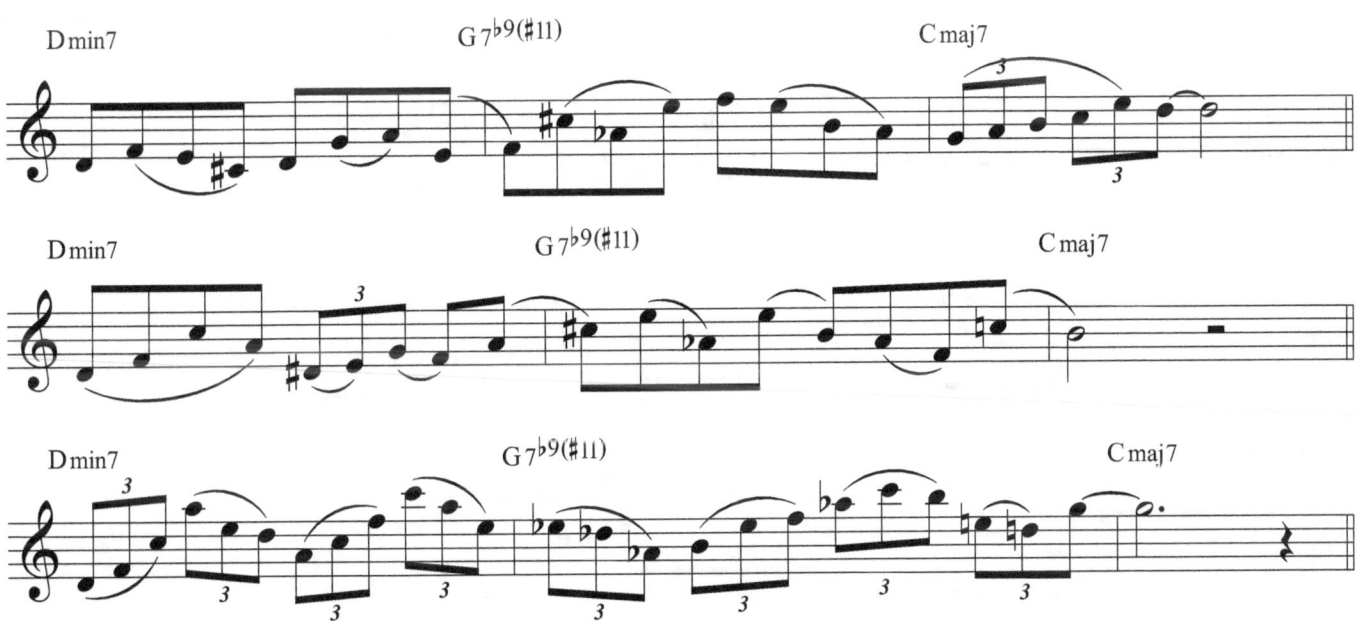

#9-#11

#11-♮13

#11-♭13

♭9-#9-♭13

♭9-#9-♭13

♭9-#11-♮13

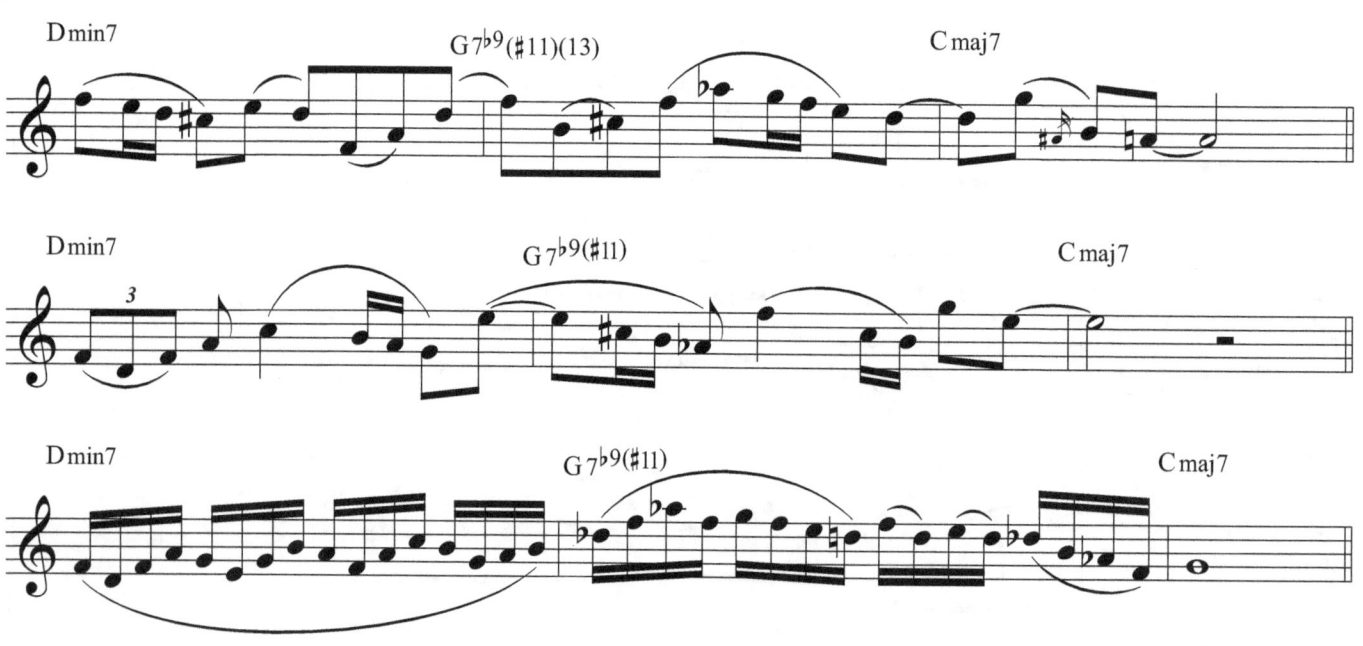

♮9-#11-♭13

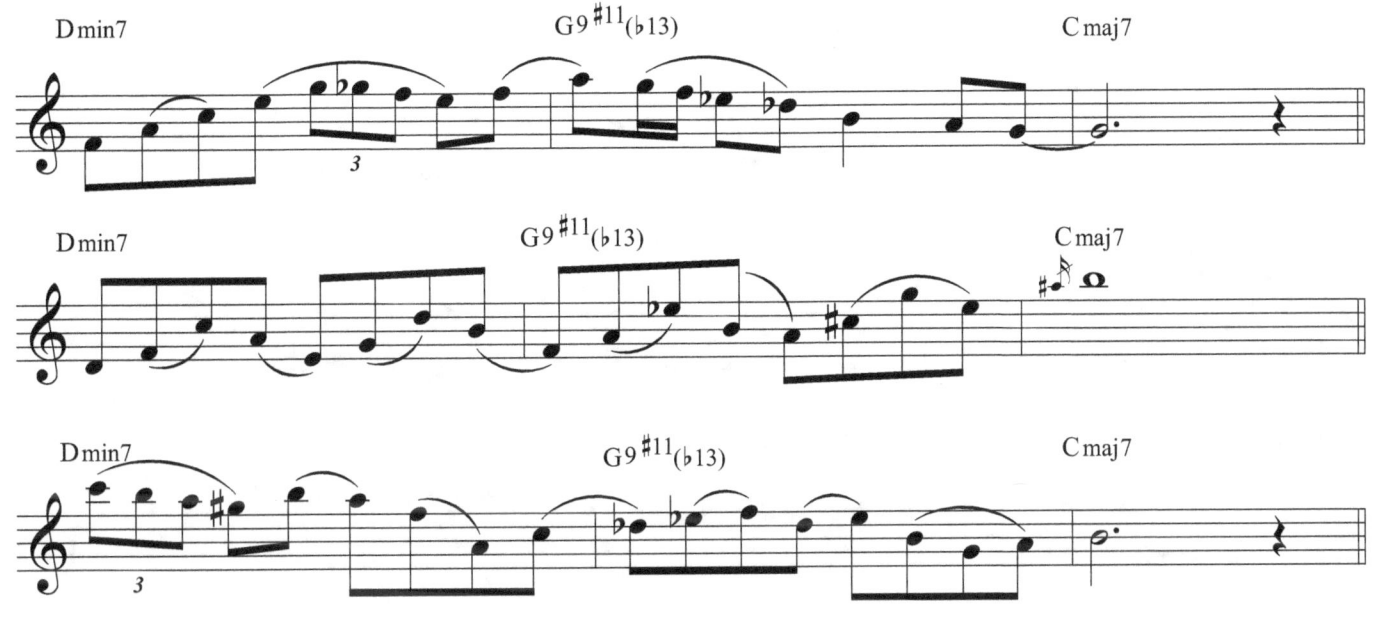

♮9-#11-♭13

♭9 - #11 - ♭13

#9 - #11 - ♮13

#9 - ♭11 - ♭13

Altered

Db MAJOR

#9-♮13

♭9-♮13

#9-♮13

#9-♭13

♭9 - ♭13

#9 - ♭13

#9-#11

b9-#11

#9-#11

#11-♮13

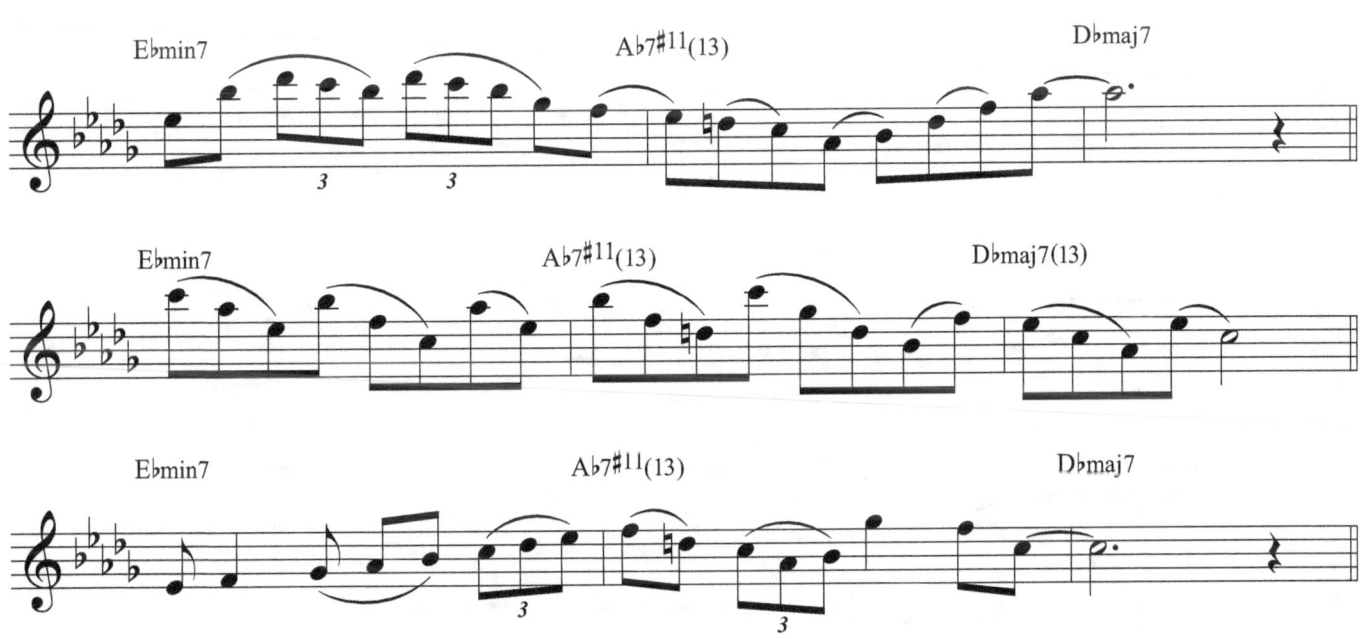

#11 - ♭13

♭9 - #9 - ♮13

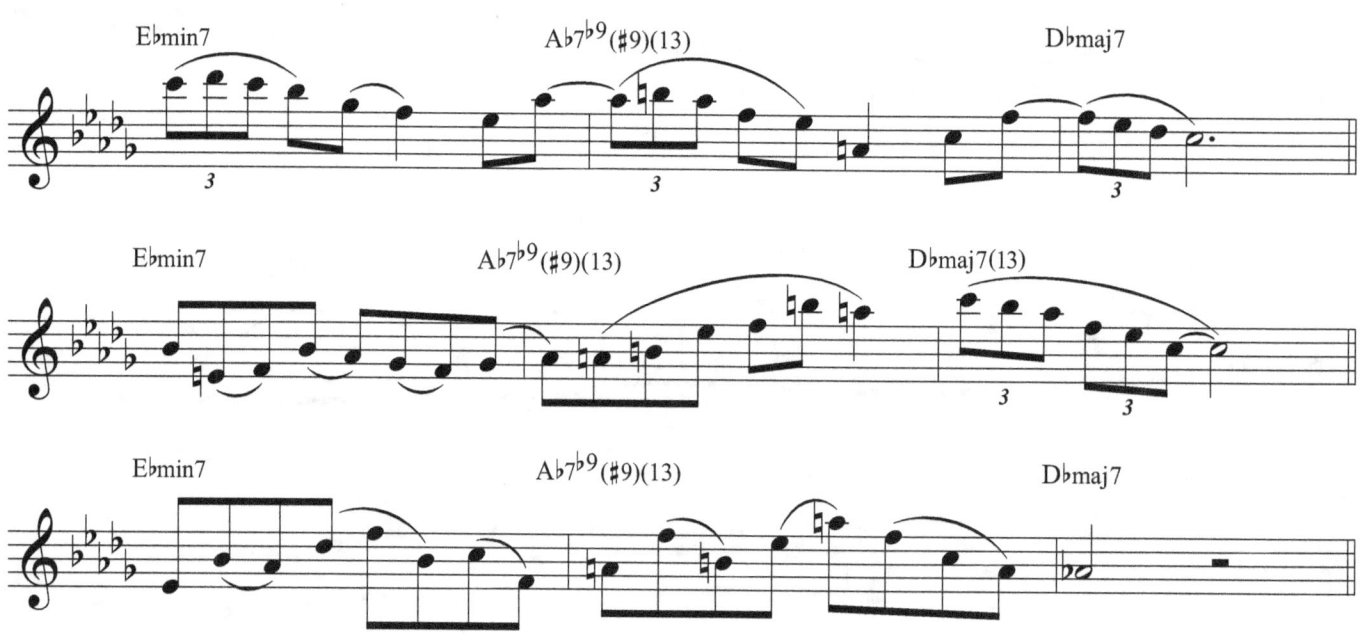

- 26 -

♭9-♯9-♭13

♭9-♯11-♮13

♭9-#11-♭13

#9-#11-♮13

#9-♭11-♭13

Altered

D MAJOR

♮9 - ♮13 (Diatonic tensions)

♭9 - ♮13

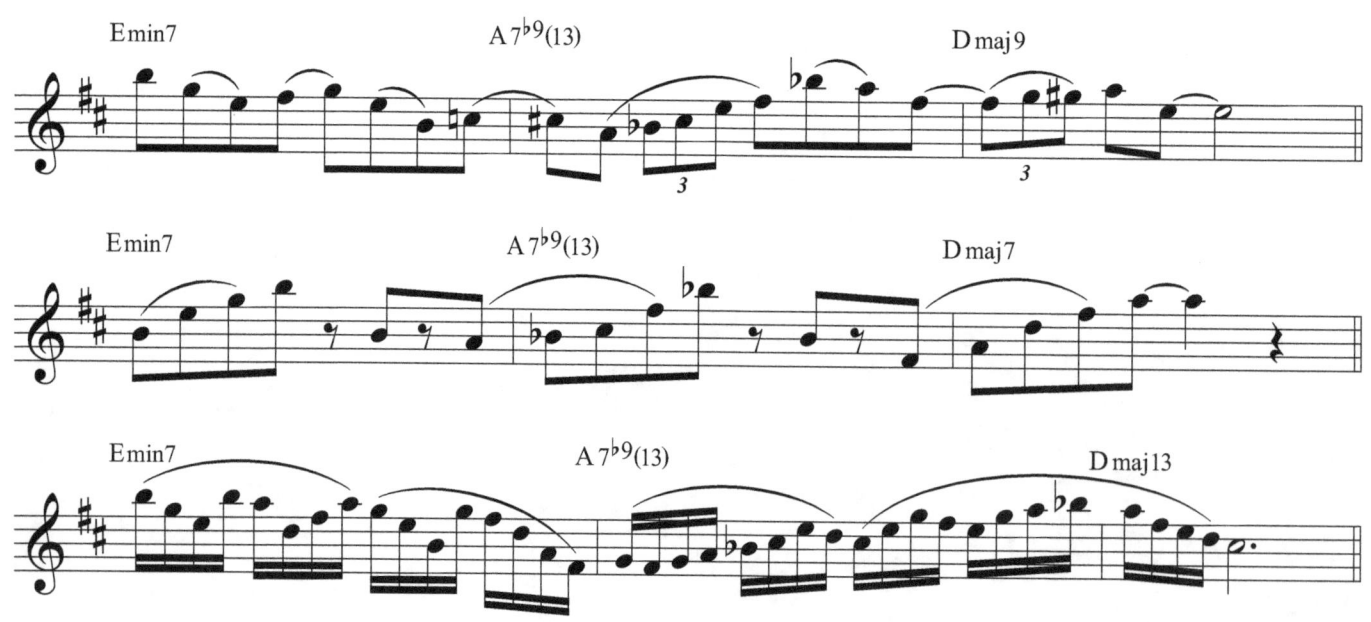

#9-♮13

♮9-♭13

♭9 - ♭13

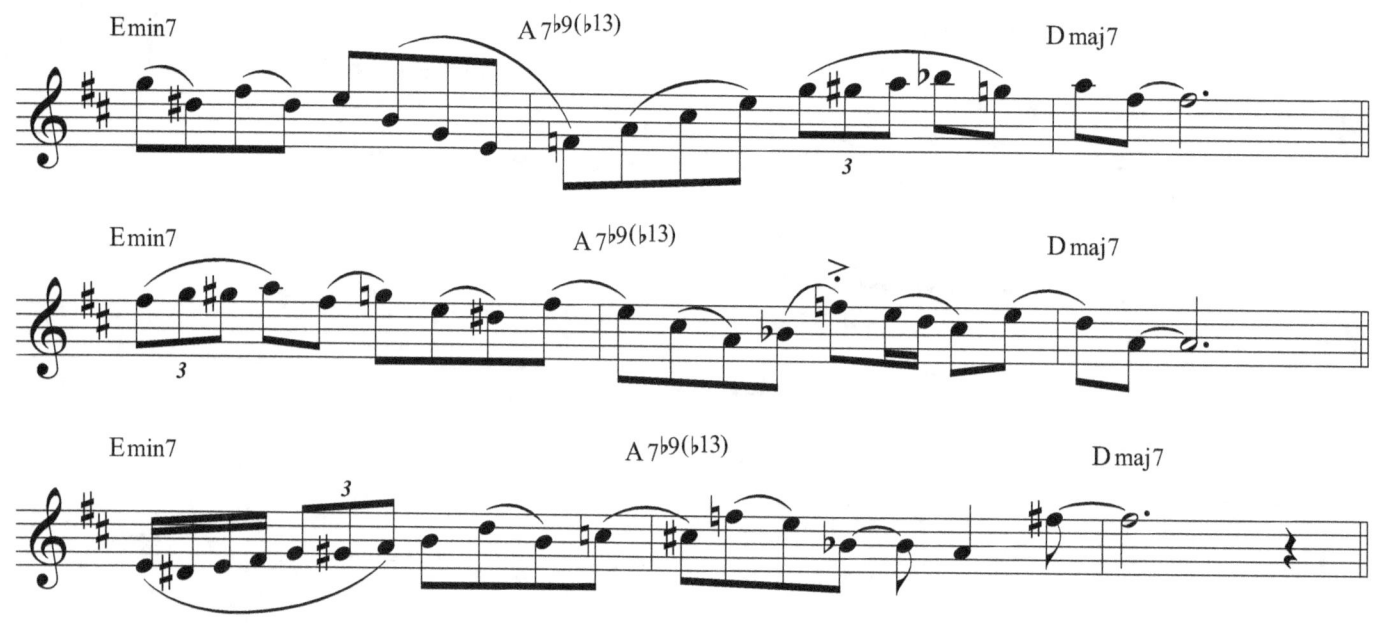

#9 - ♭13

♮9-#11

♭9-#11

#9-#11

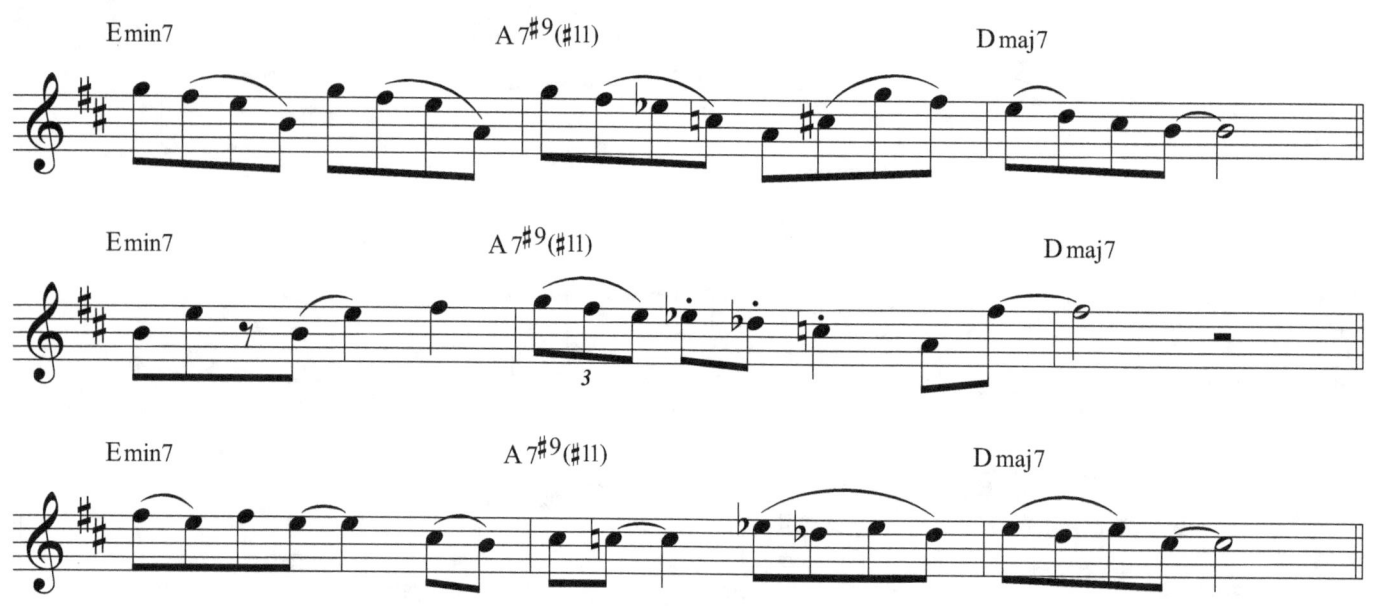

#11-♮13

#11-♭13

♭9-#9-♮13

♭9-♯9-♭13

♭9-♯11-♮13

♮9-♯11-♭13

♮9-♯11-♮13

♭9 - #11 - ♭13

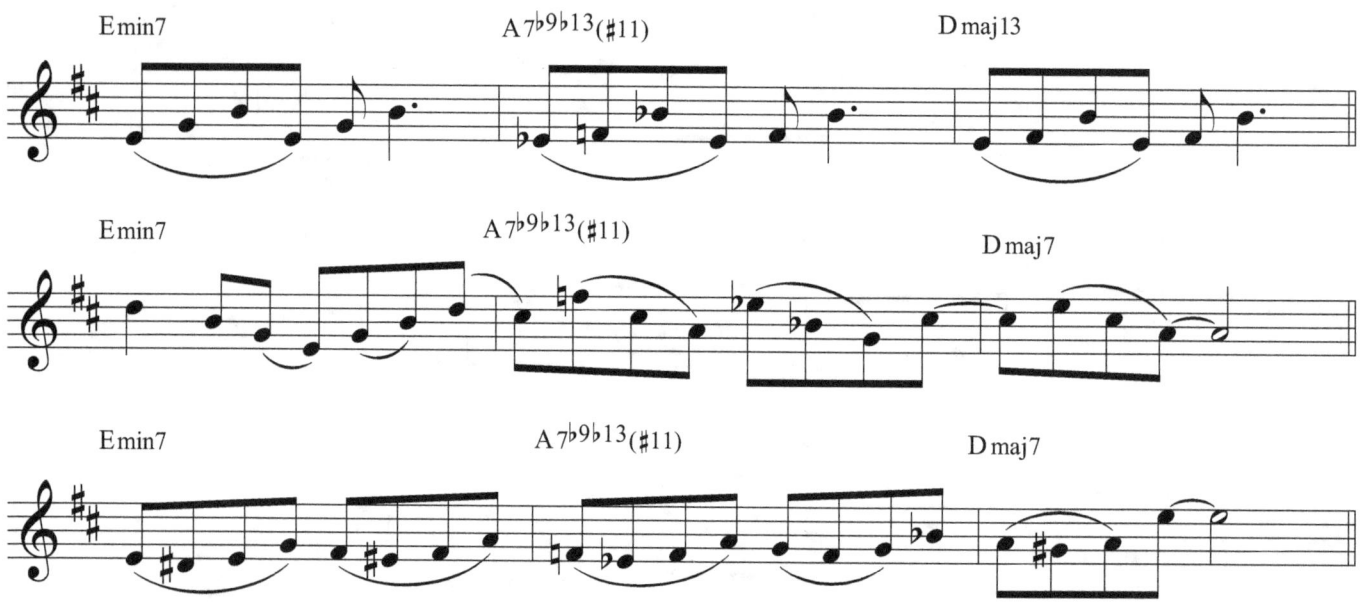

#9 - #11 - ♭13

#9-♭11-♭13

Altered

EB MAJOR

♮9 - ♮13 (Diatonic tensions)

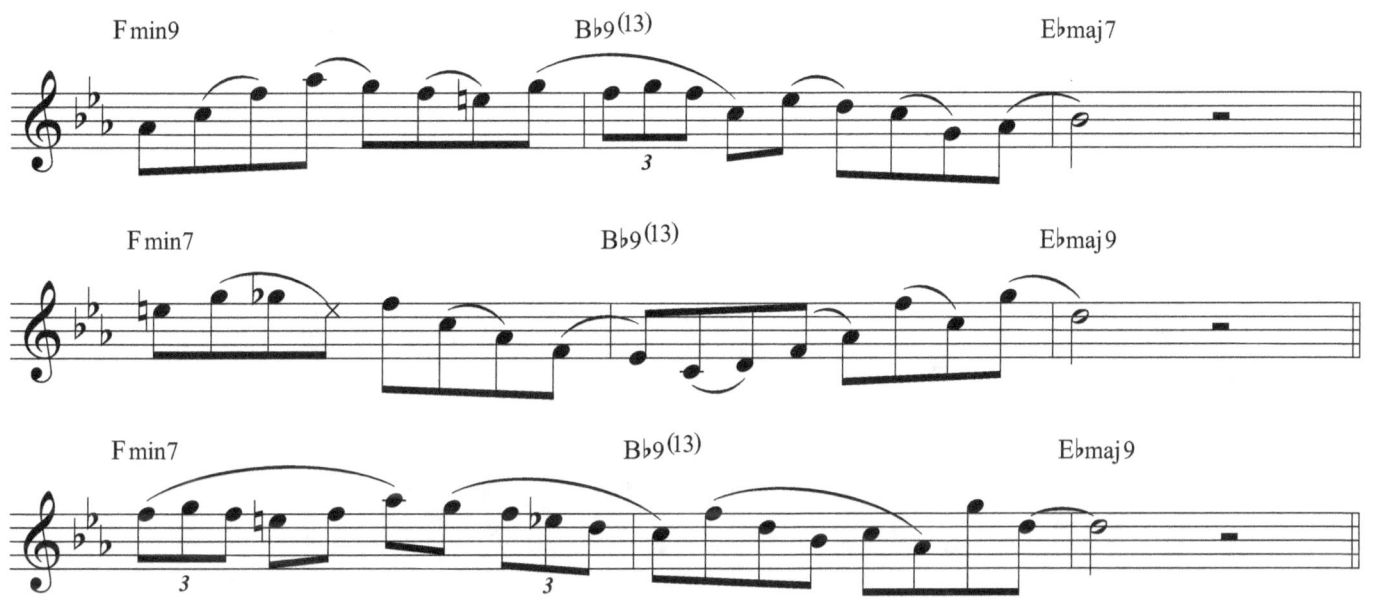

♭9 - ♮13

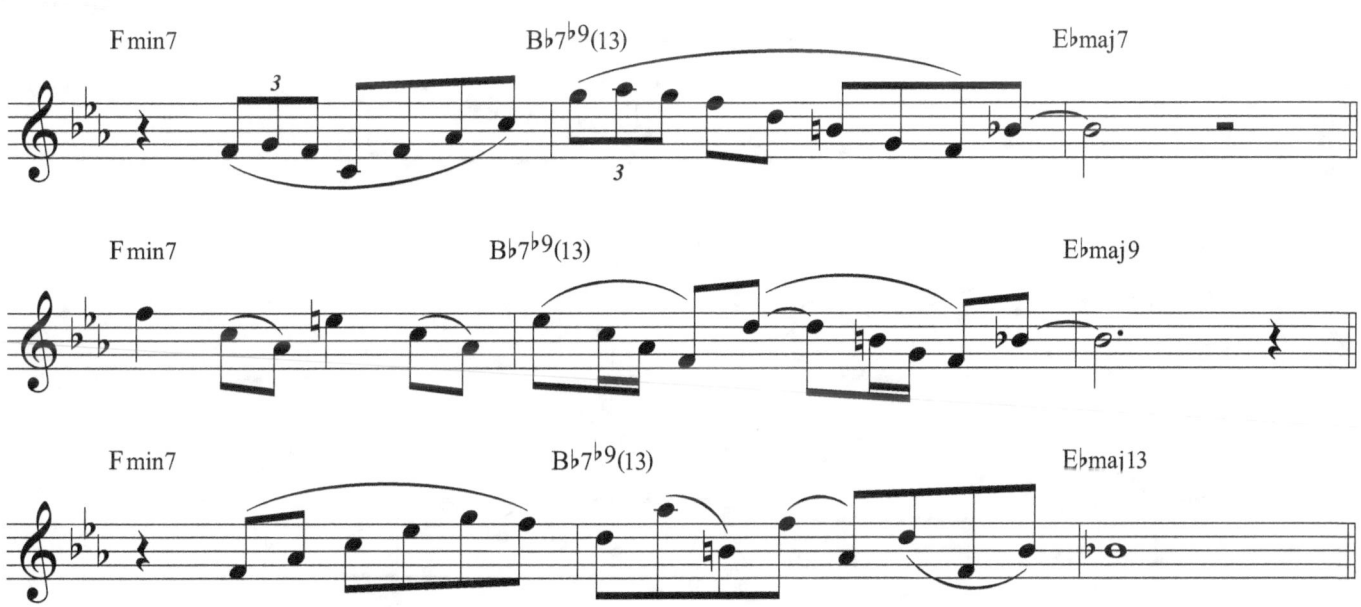

#9-♮13

♮9-♭13

♭9 - ♭13

#9 - ♭13

♭9-#11

♭9-#11

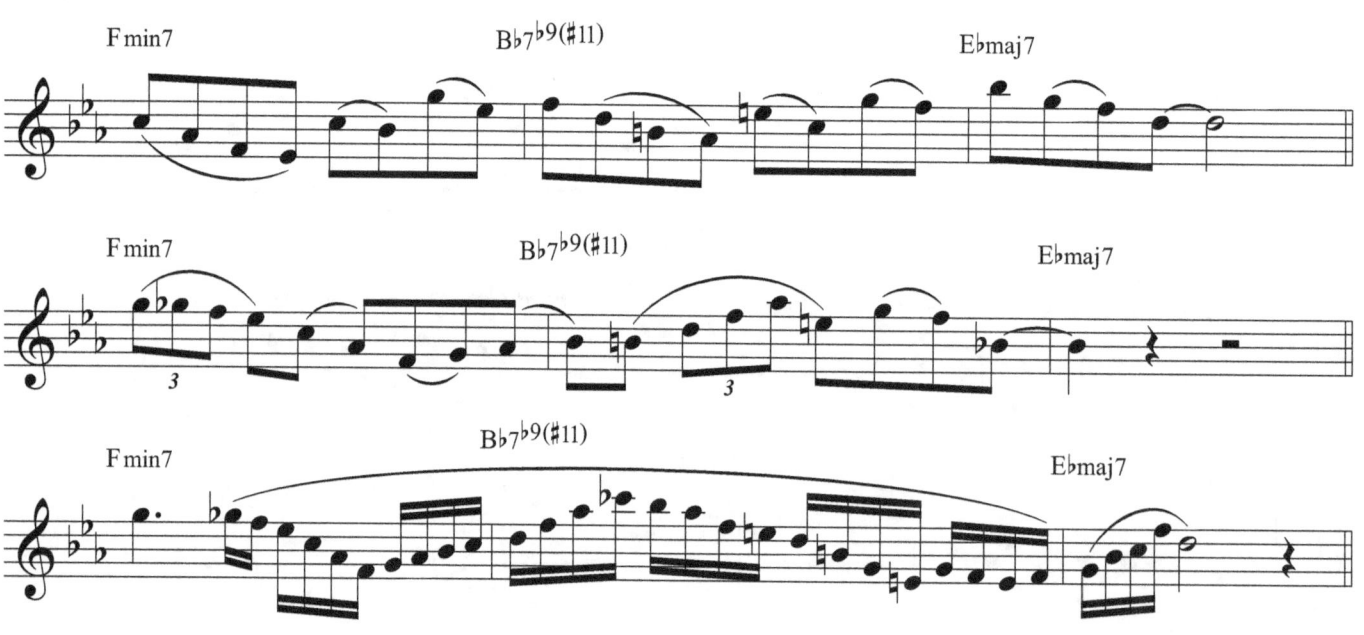

#9-#11

#11-♮13

#11 - ♭13

♭9 - #9 - ♮13

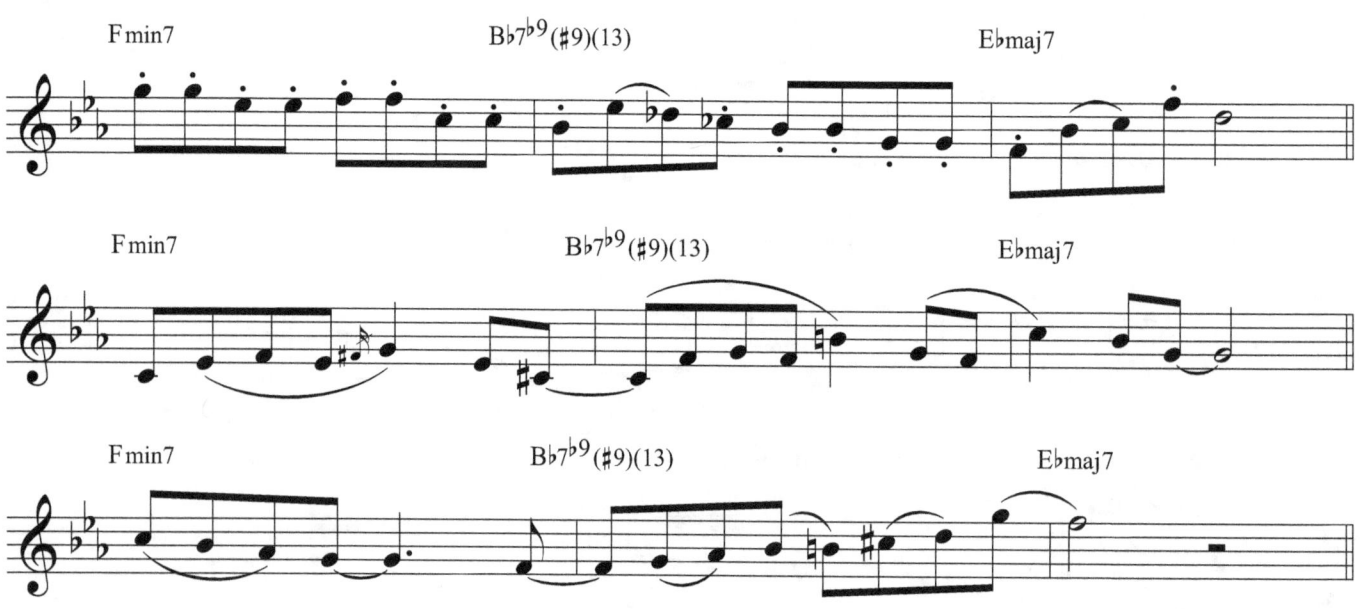

♭9-#9-♭13

♭9-#11-♮13

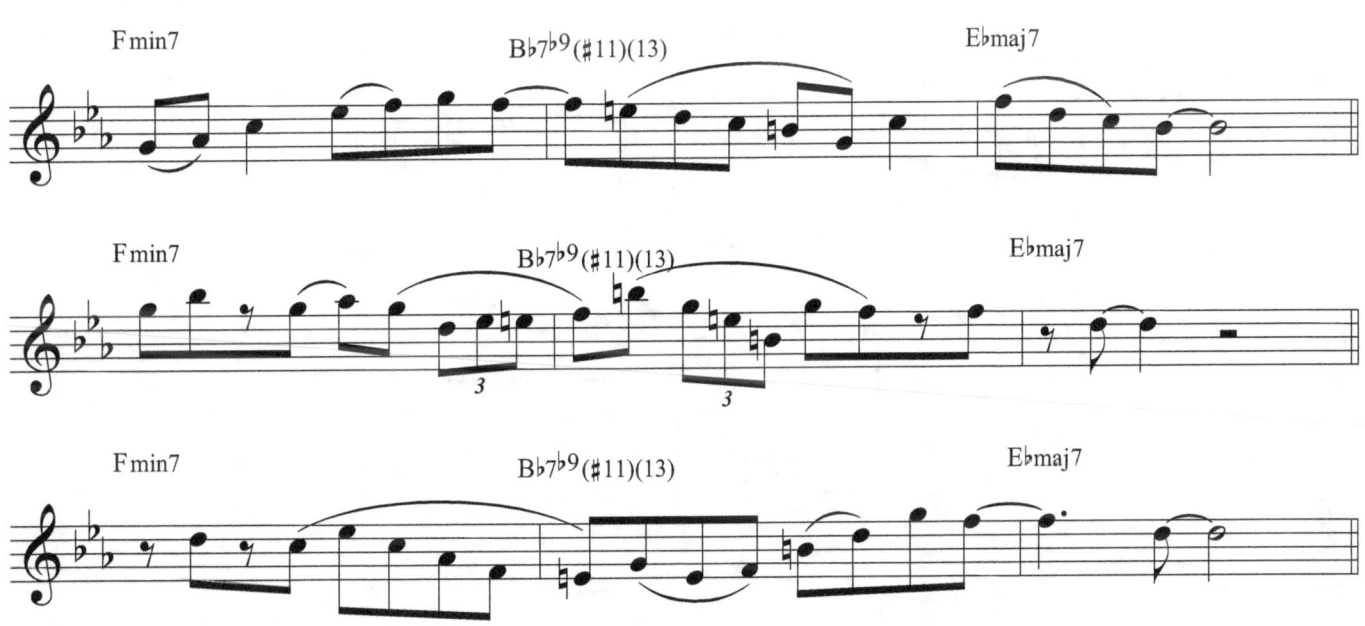

♮9-#11-♭13

♮9-#11-♮13

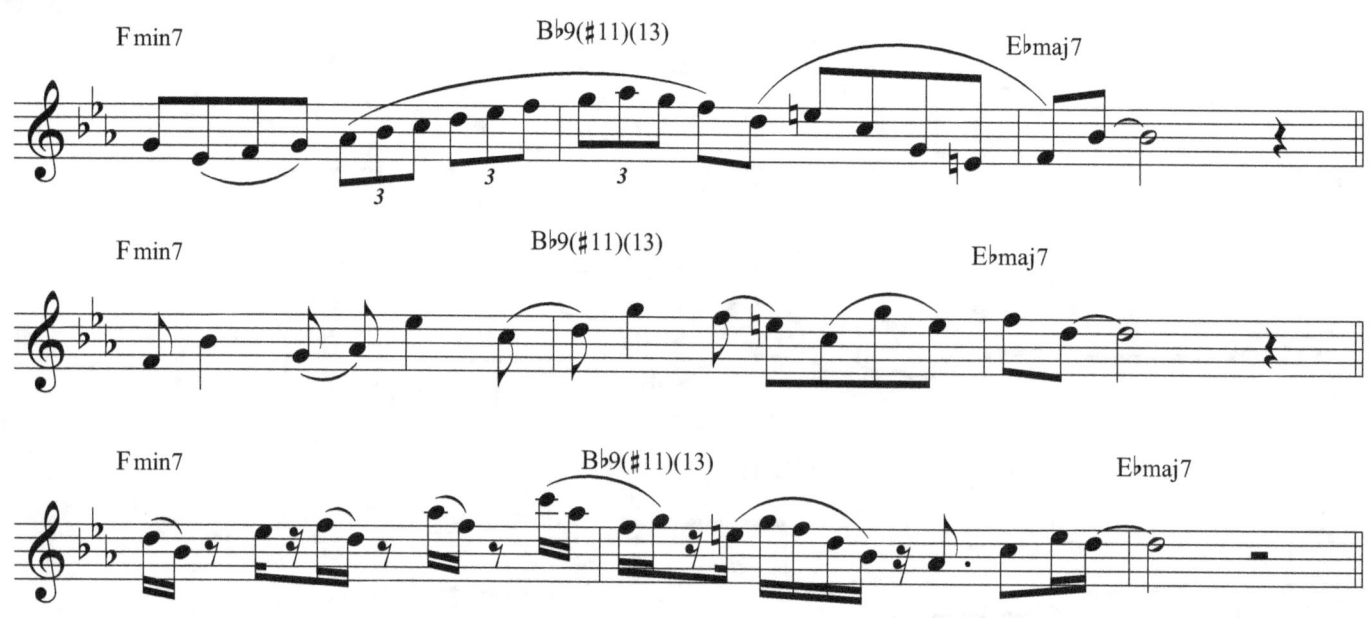

♭9-♯11-♭13

♯9-♯11-♭13

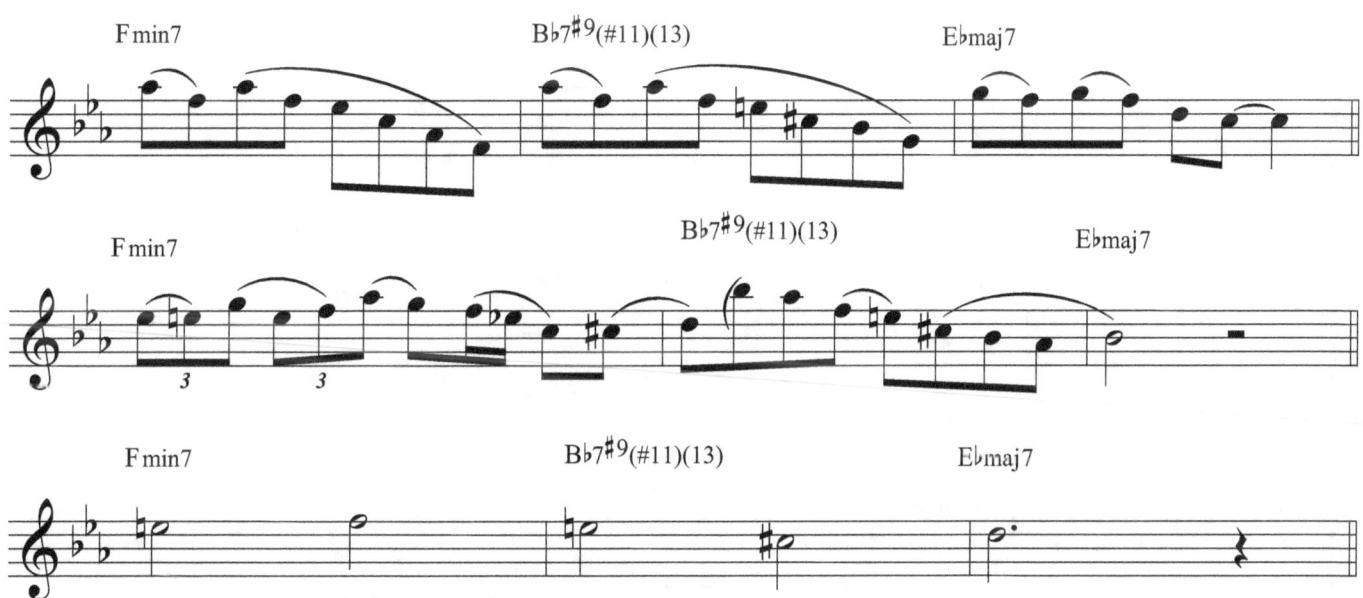

#9-♭11-♭13

Altered

E MAJOR

♮9 - ♮13 (Diatonic tensions)

♭9 - ♮13

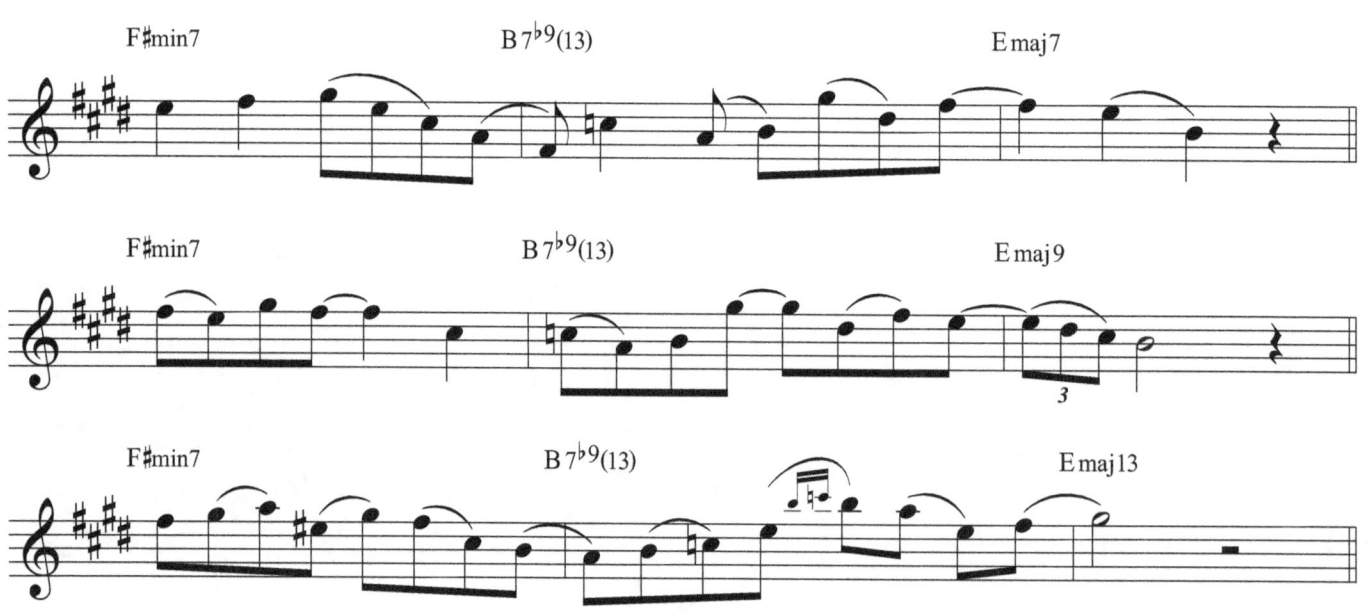

#9-♮13

♮9-♭13

♭9 - ♭13

#9 - ♭13

♮9-#11

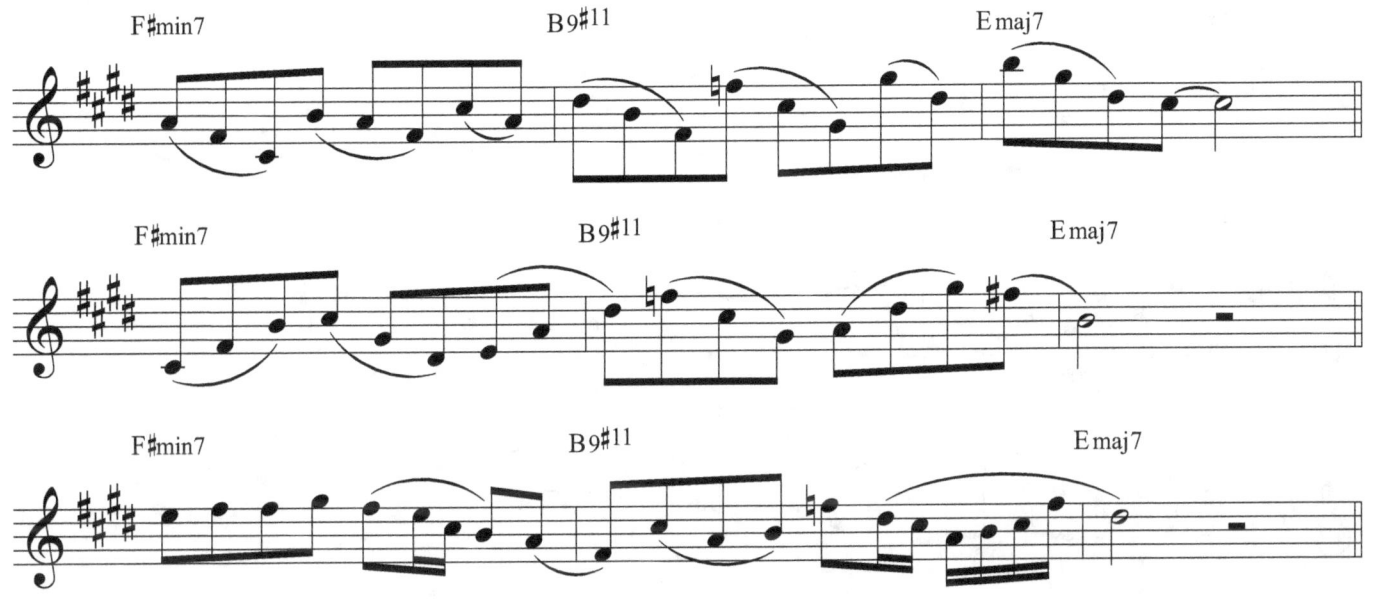

♭9-#11

#9-#11

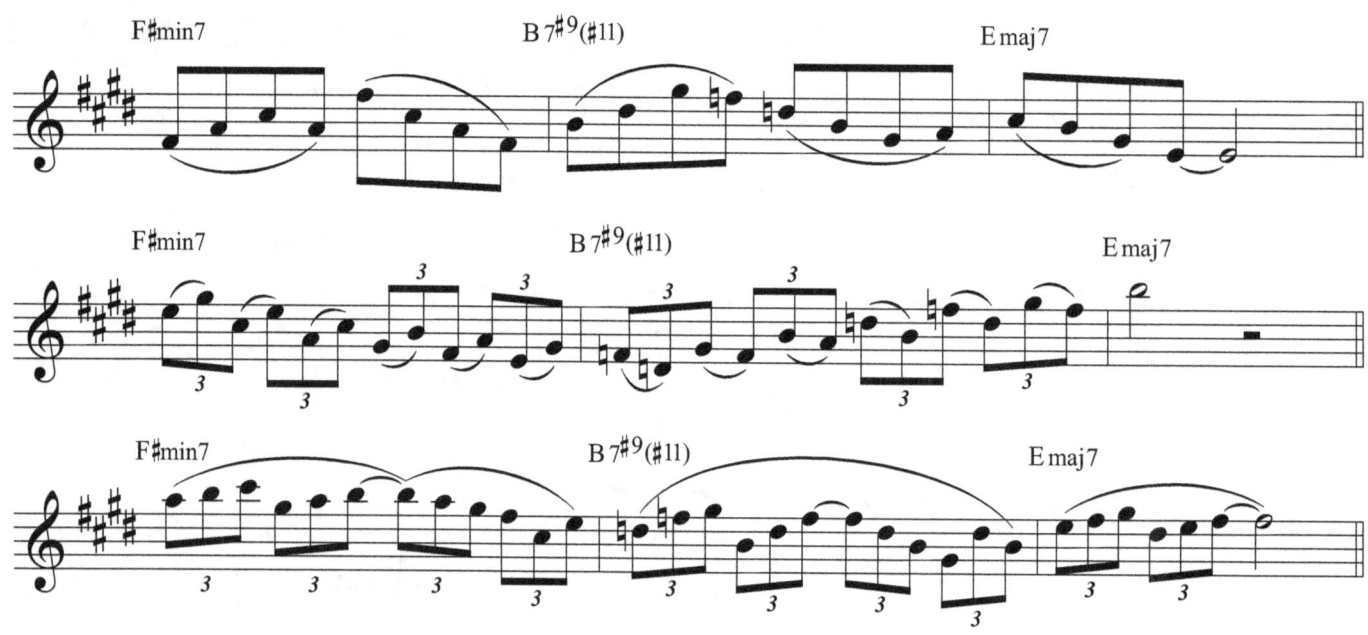

#11-♭13

#11 - ♭13

♭9 - #9 - ♮13

♭9-♯9-♭13

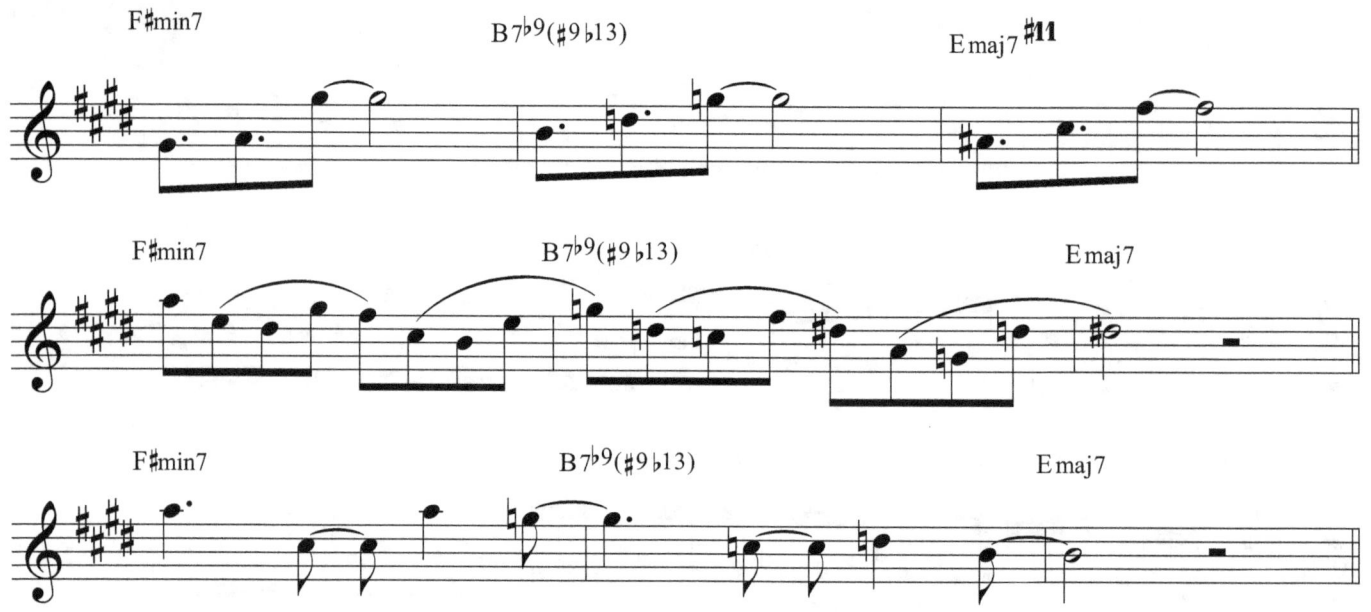

♭9-♯11-♮13

♮9-#11-♭13

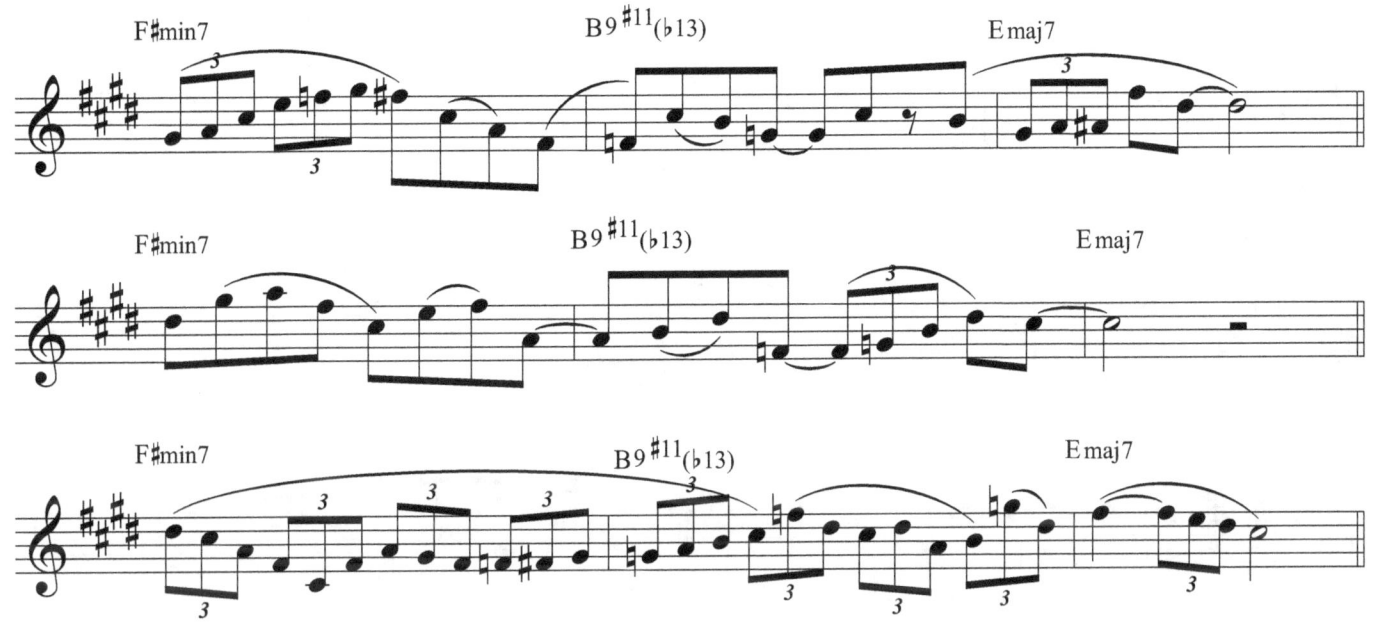

♮9-#11-♭13

♭9-#11-♭13

#9-#11-♮13

#9 - ♭11 - ♭13

Altered

F MAJOR

♮9 - ♮13 (Diatonic tensions)

♭9 - ♮13

#9-♮13

♮9-♭13

♭9 - ♭13

#9 - ♭13

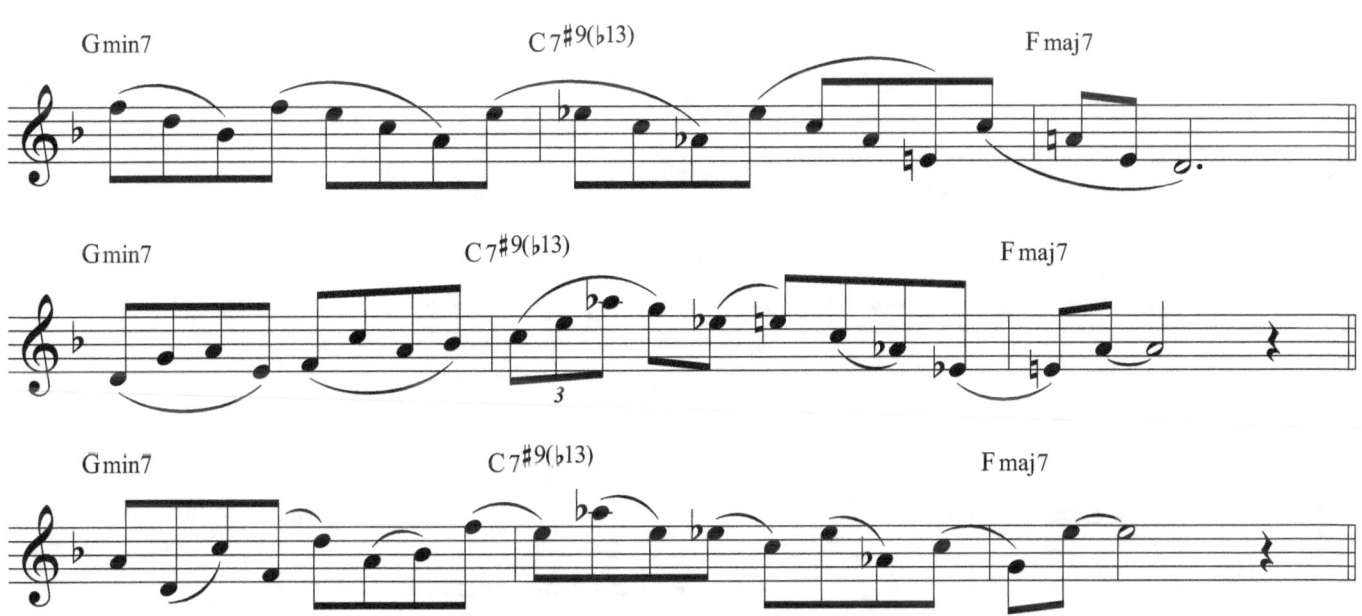

♭9-#11

♭9-#11

#9-#11

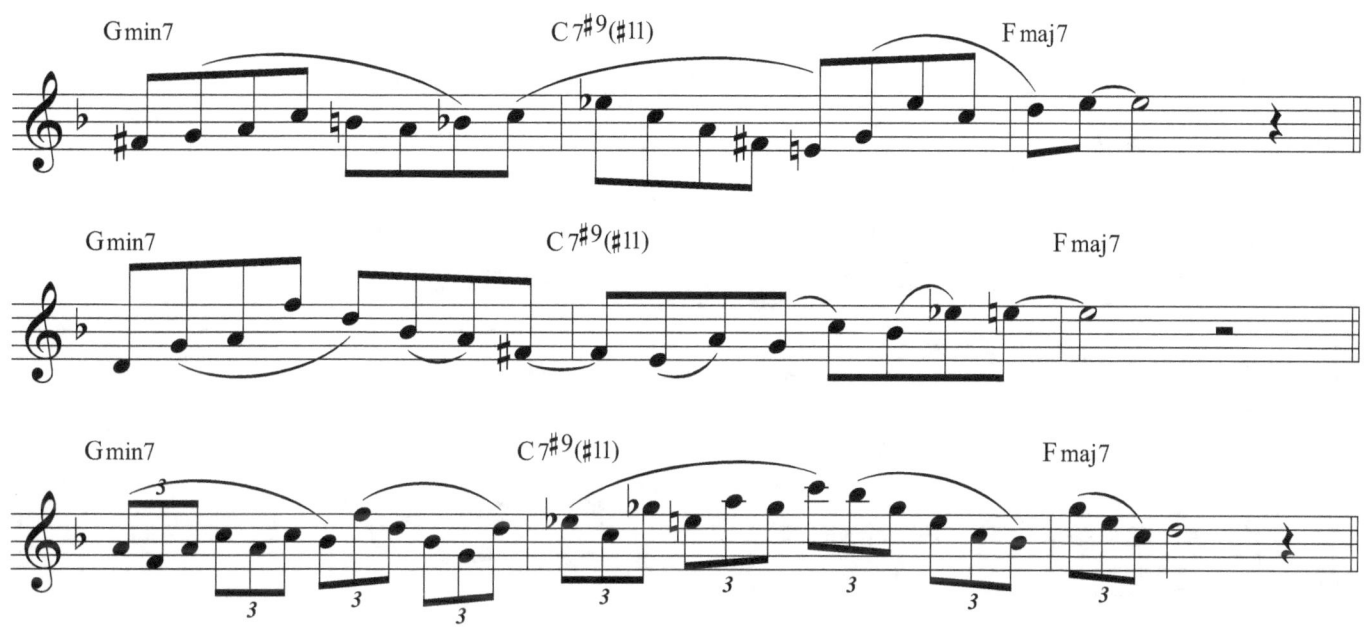

#11-♭13

#11 - ♭13

♭9 - #9 - ♭13

♭9-♯9-♭13

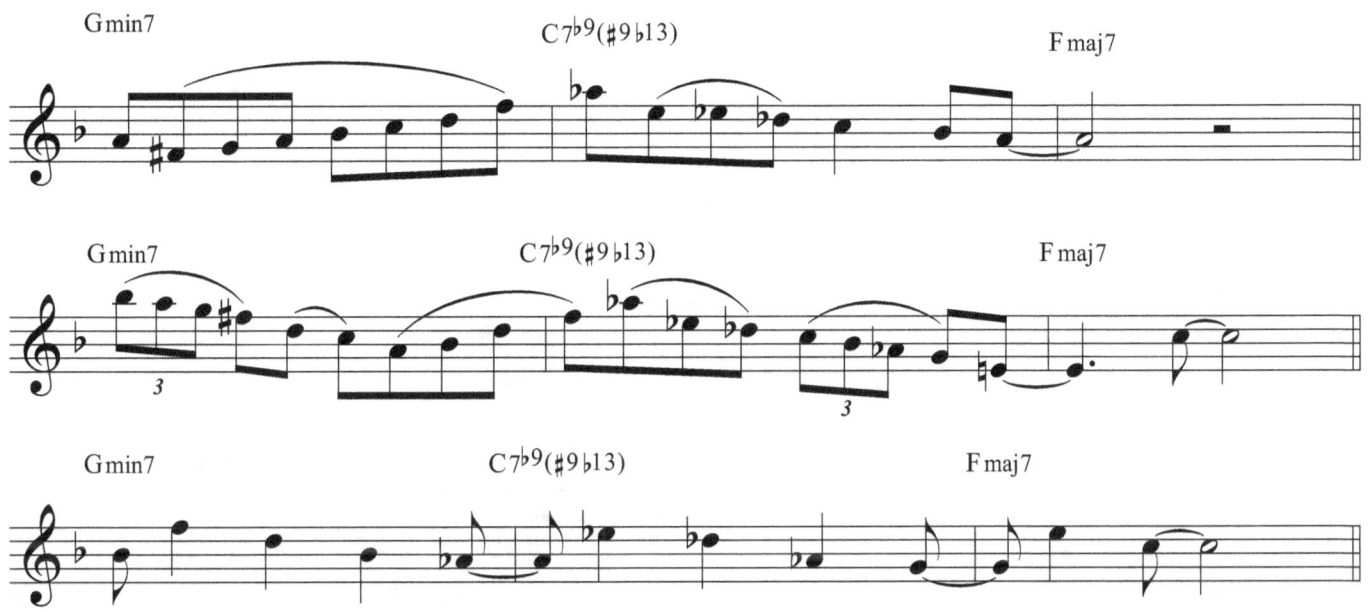

♭9-♯11-♭13

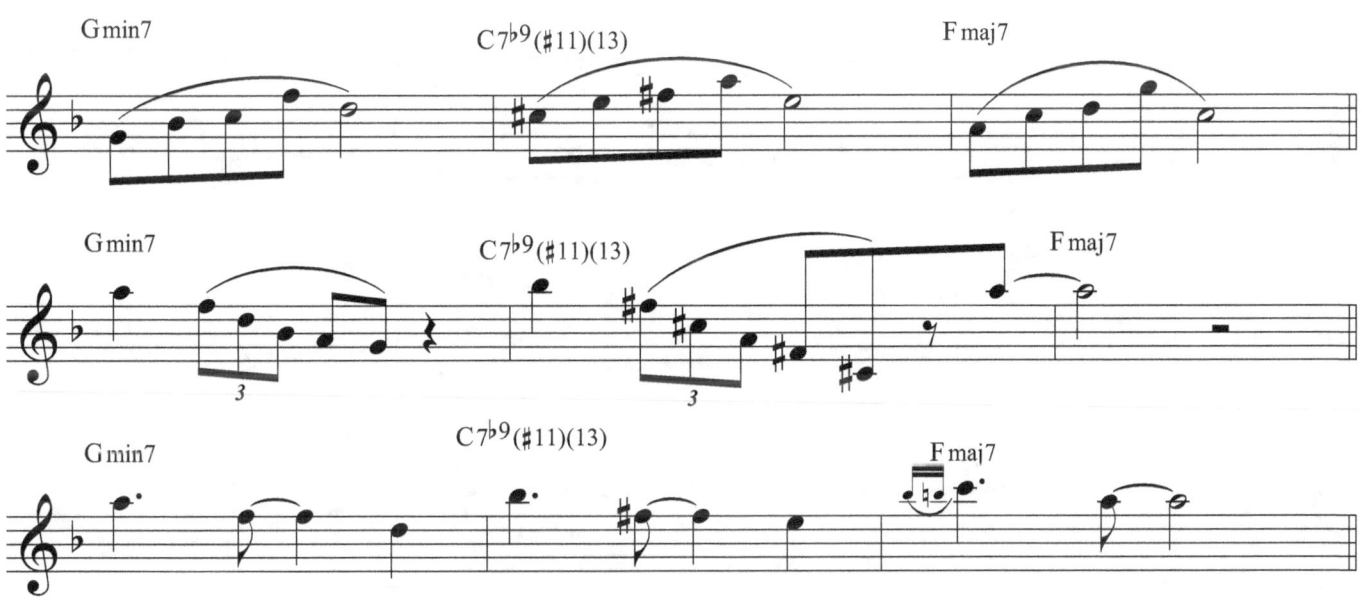

♮9-♯11-♭13

♮9-♯11-♮13

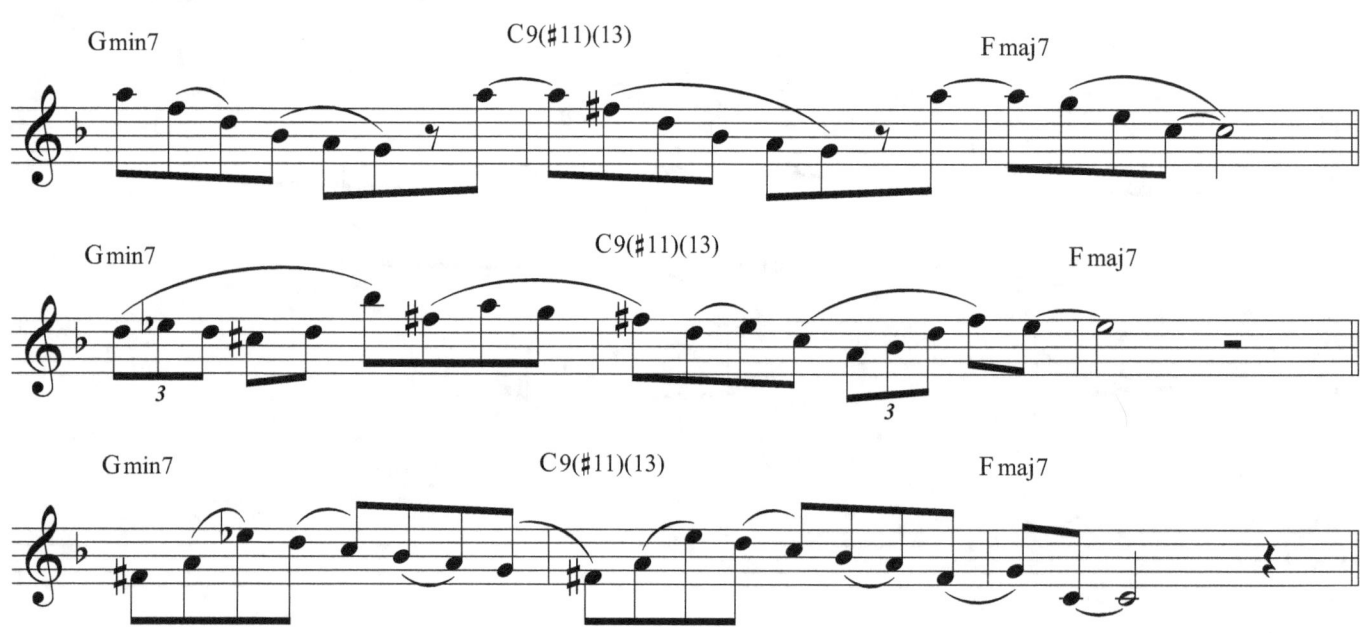

♭9-#11-♭13

#9-#11-♮13

#9-♭11-♭13

Altered

F# MAJOR

♮9 - ♮13 (Diatonic tensions)

♭9 - ♮13

#9-♮13

♮9-♭13

♭9 - ♭13

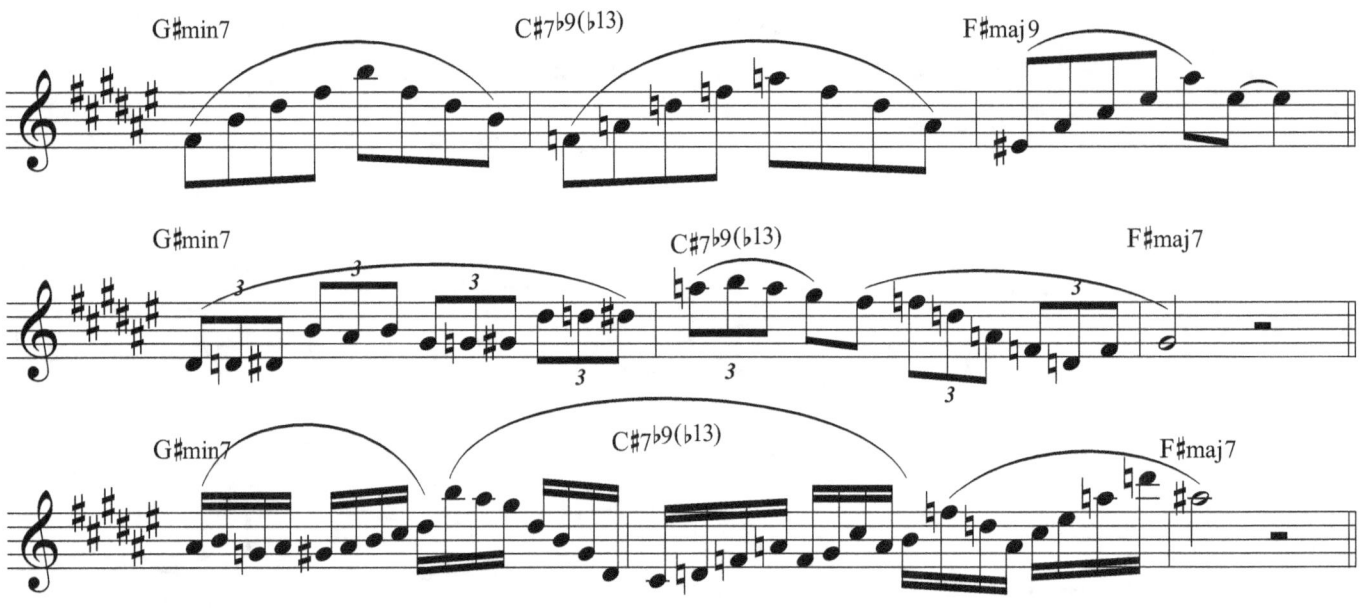

♯9 - ♭13

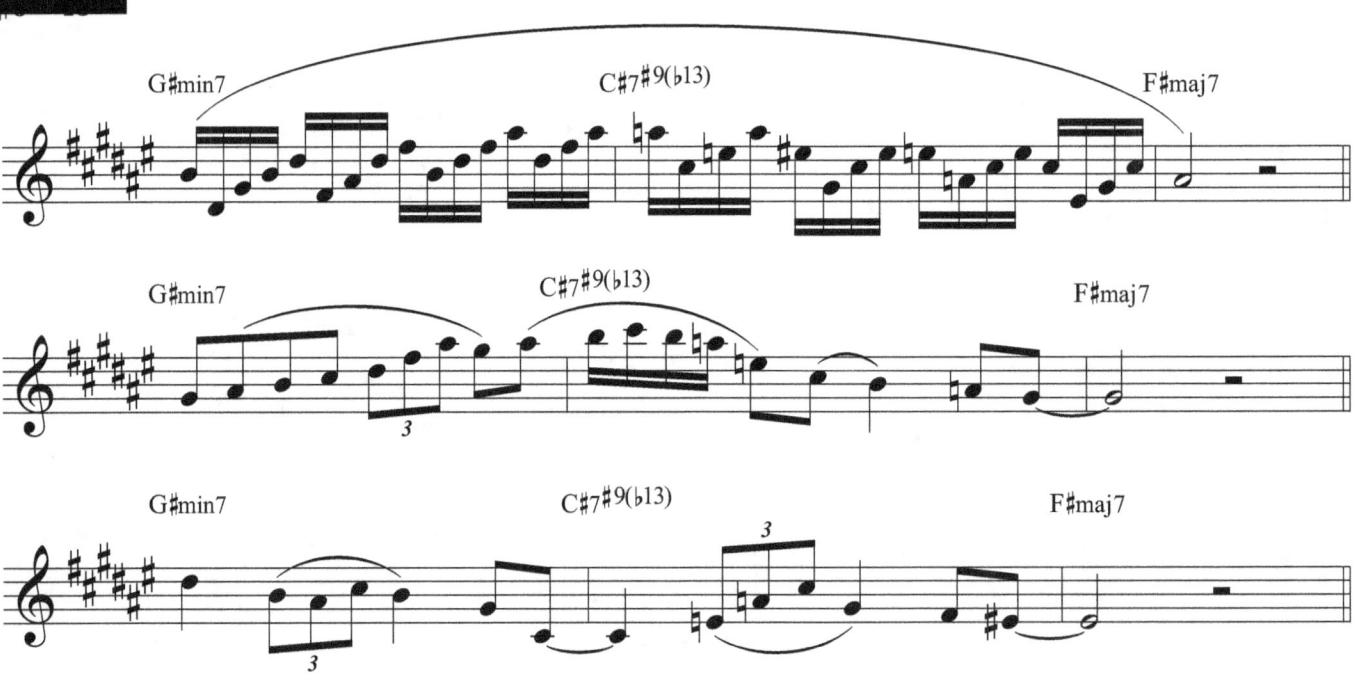

♮9-#11

♭9-#11

#9-#11

#11-♭13

#11 - ♭13

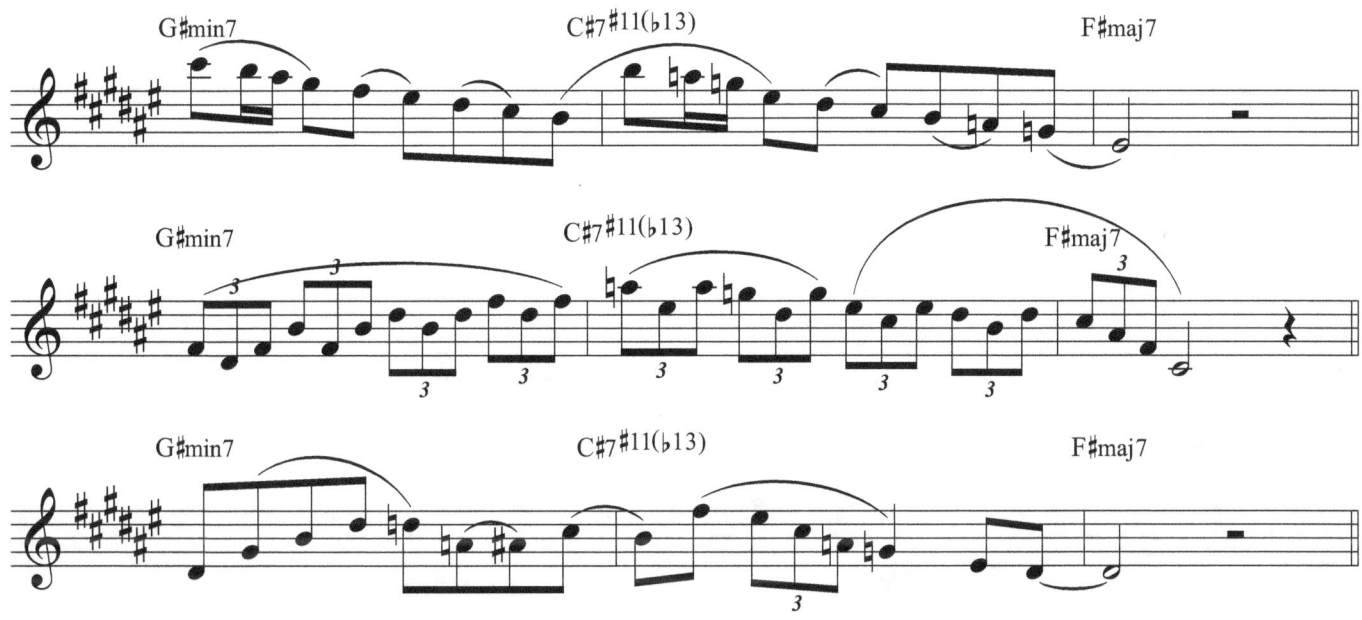

♭9 - #9 - ♭13

♭9-#9-♭13

♭9-#11-♭13

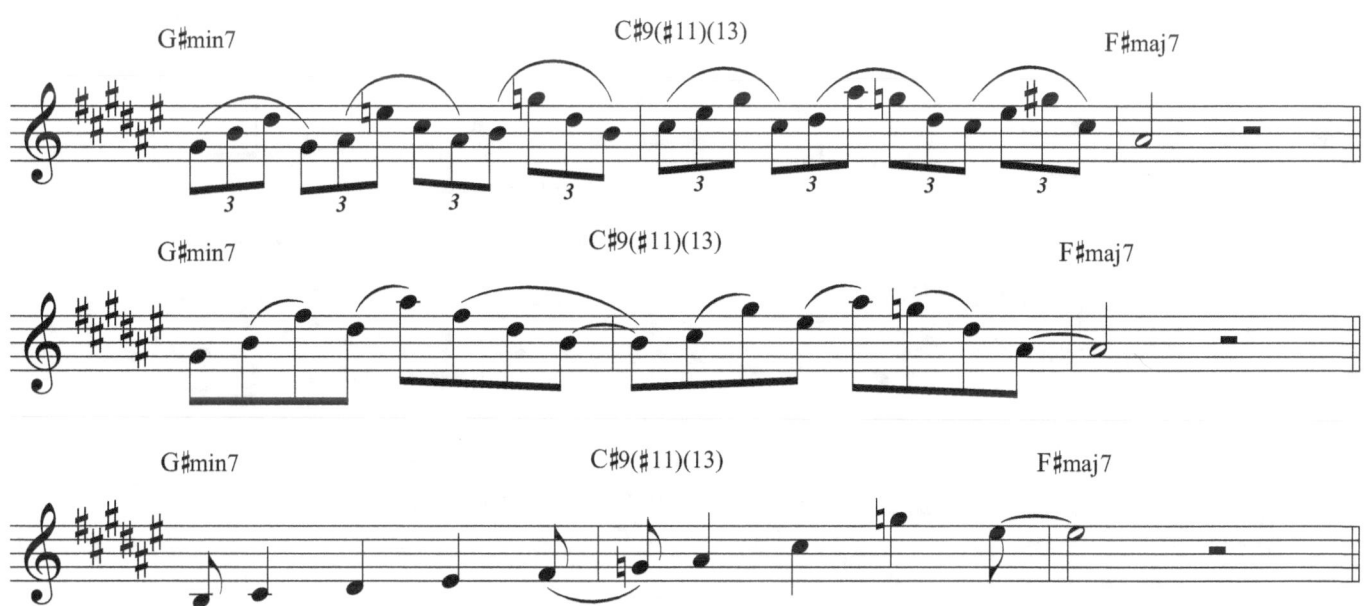

♭9-#11-♭13

#9-#11-♮13

#9-♭11-♭13

Altered

G MAJOR

♮9 - ♮13 (Diatonic tensions)

♭9 - ♮13

#9-♮13

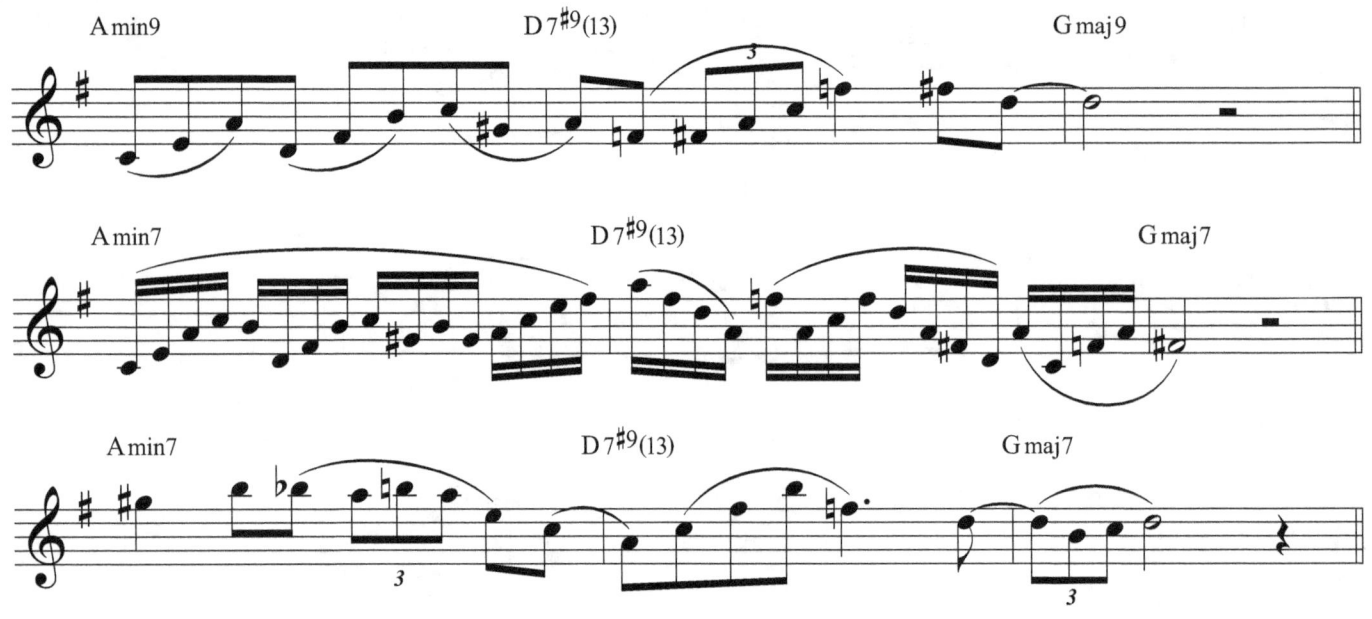

♮9-♭13

♭9 - ♭13

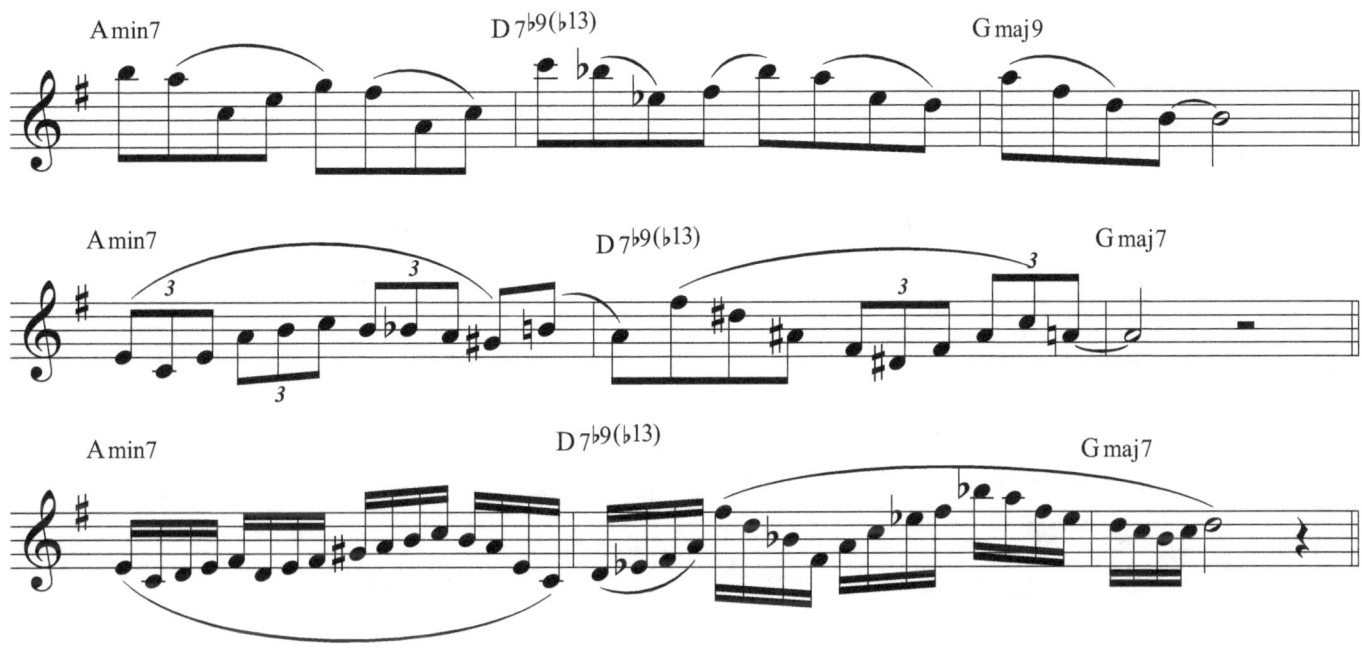

#9 - ♭13

♮9-♯11

♭9-♯11

#9-#11

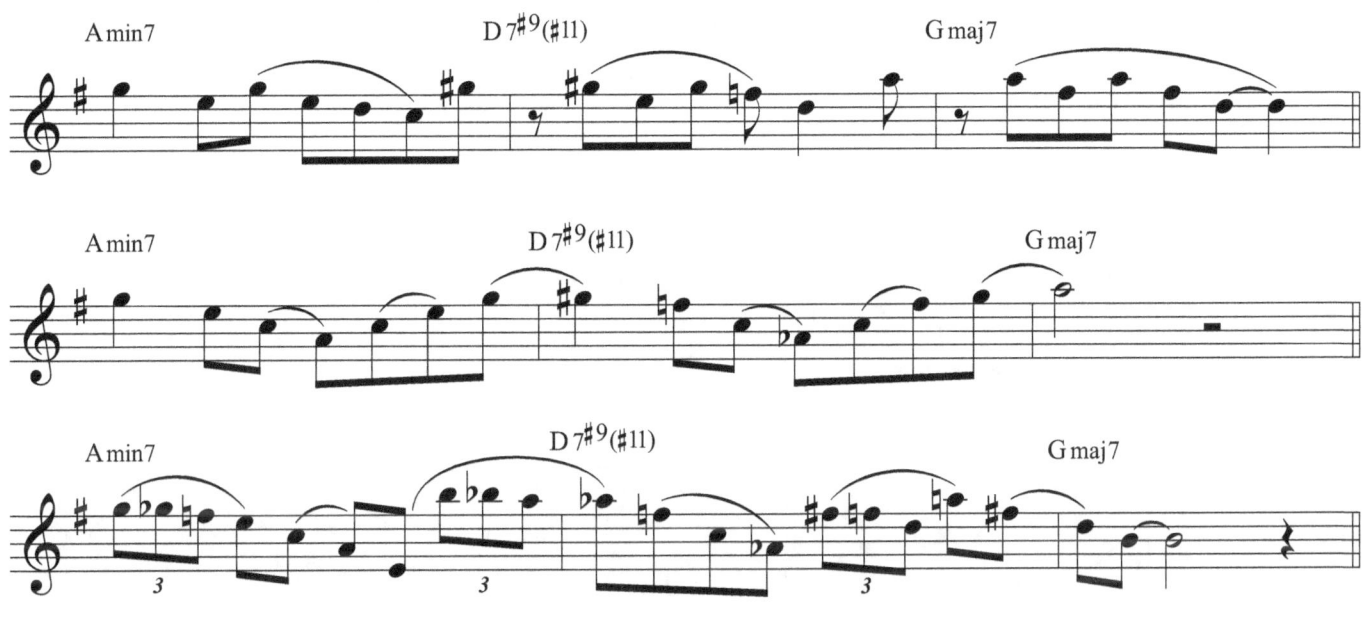

#11-♮13

#11 - ♭13

♭9 - #9 - ♮13

♭9-#9-♭13

♭9-#11-♭13

♮9-#11-♭13

♮9-#11-♭13

♭9-♯11-♭13

♯9-♯11-♮13

#9 - ♭11 - ♭13

Altered

Ab MAJOR

♮9 - ♮13 (Diatonic tensions)

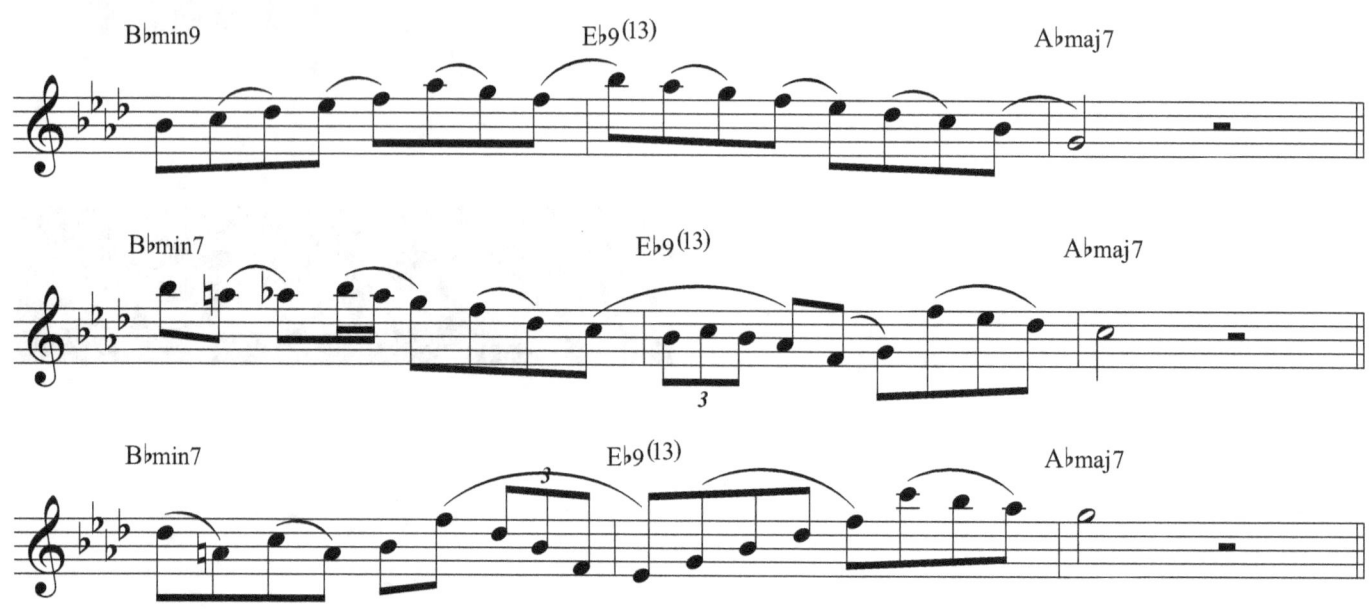

♭9 - ♮13

#9-♮13

♮9-♭13

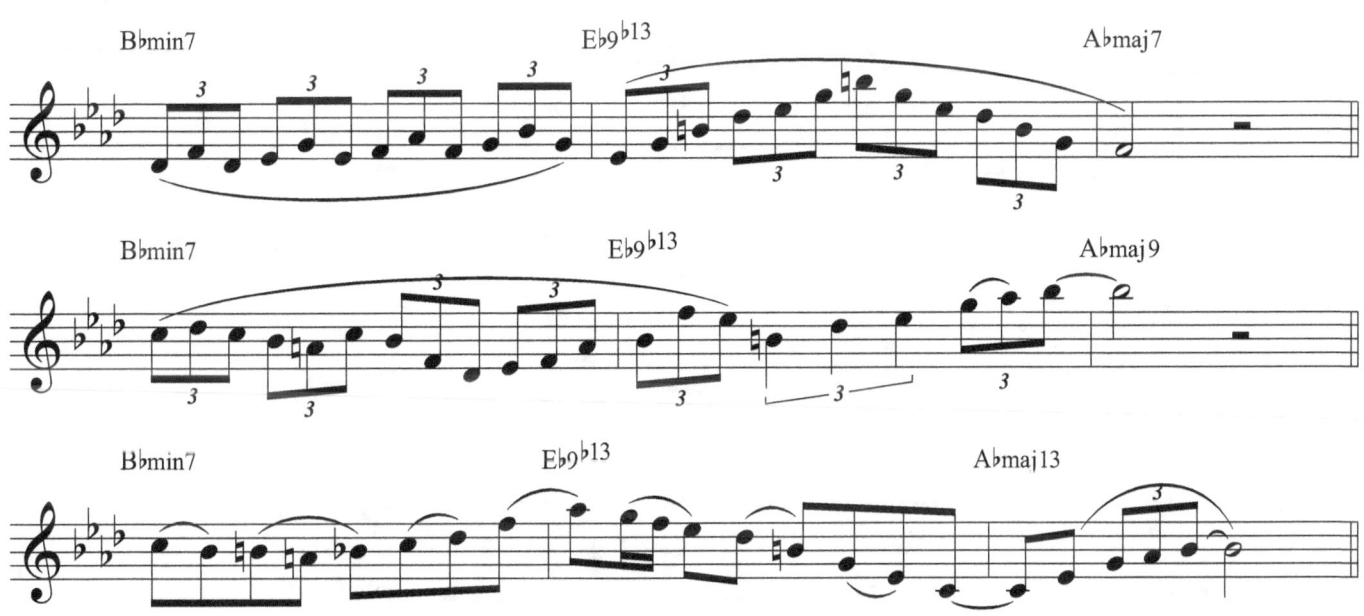

♭9 - ♭13

#9 - ♭13

♮9-#11

♭9-#11

#9-#11

#11-♮13

#11 - b13

b9 - #9 - b13

♭9-♯9-♭13

♭9-♯11-♮13

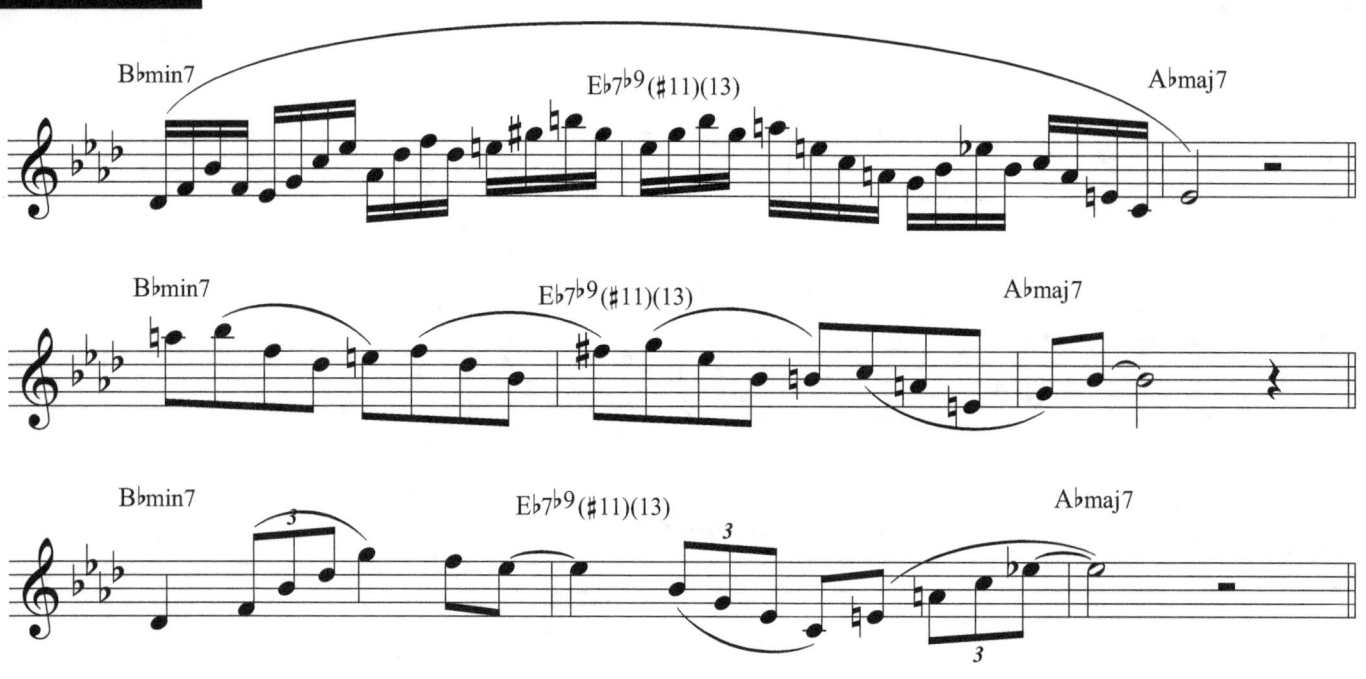

♮9 - #11 - ♭13

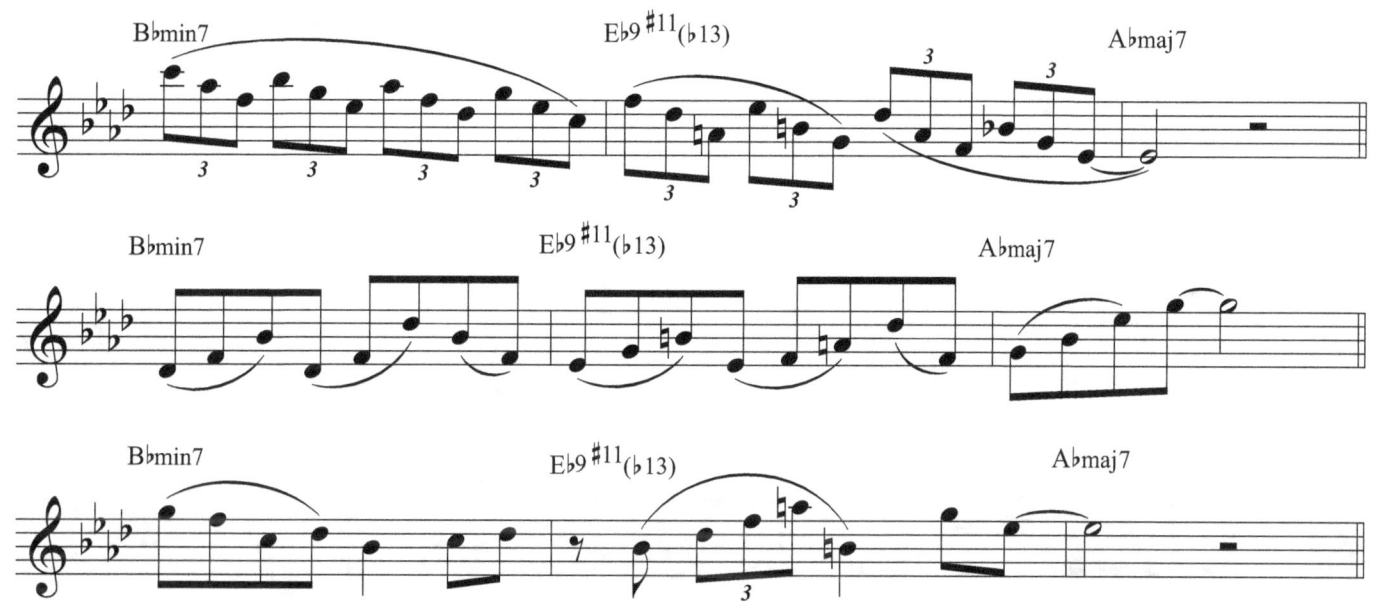

♮9 - #11 - ♮13

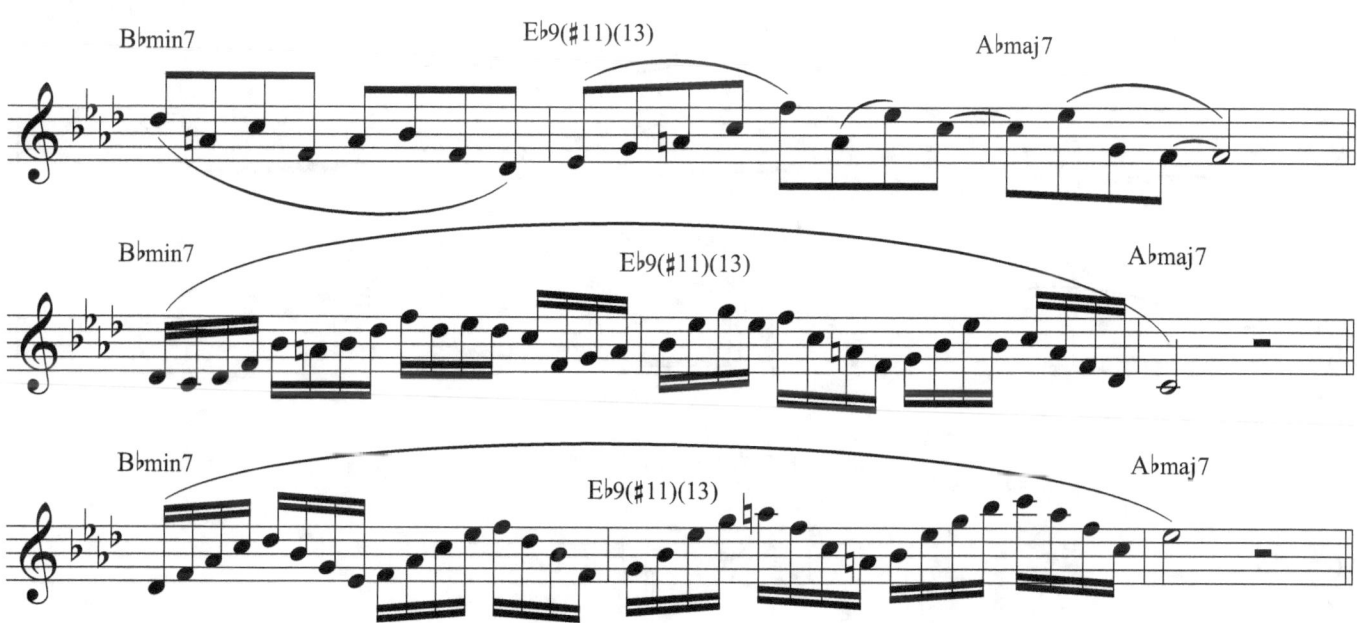

♭9-♯11-♭13

♯9-♯11-♭13

#9-♭11-♭13

Altered

A MAJOR

♮9 - ♮13 (Diatonic tensions)

♭9 - ♮13

#9-♮13

♮9-♭13

♭9 - ♭13

♯9 - ♭13

#9-#11

#11-♮13

#11 - ♭13

♭9 - #9 - ♭13

♭9-♯9-♭13

♭9-♯11-♮13

♮9-#11-♭13

♮9-#11-♭13

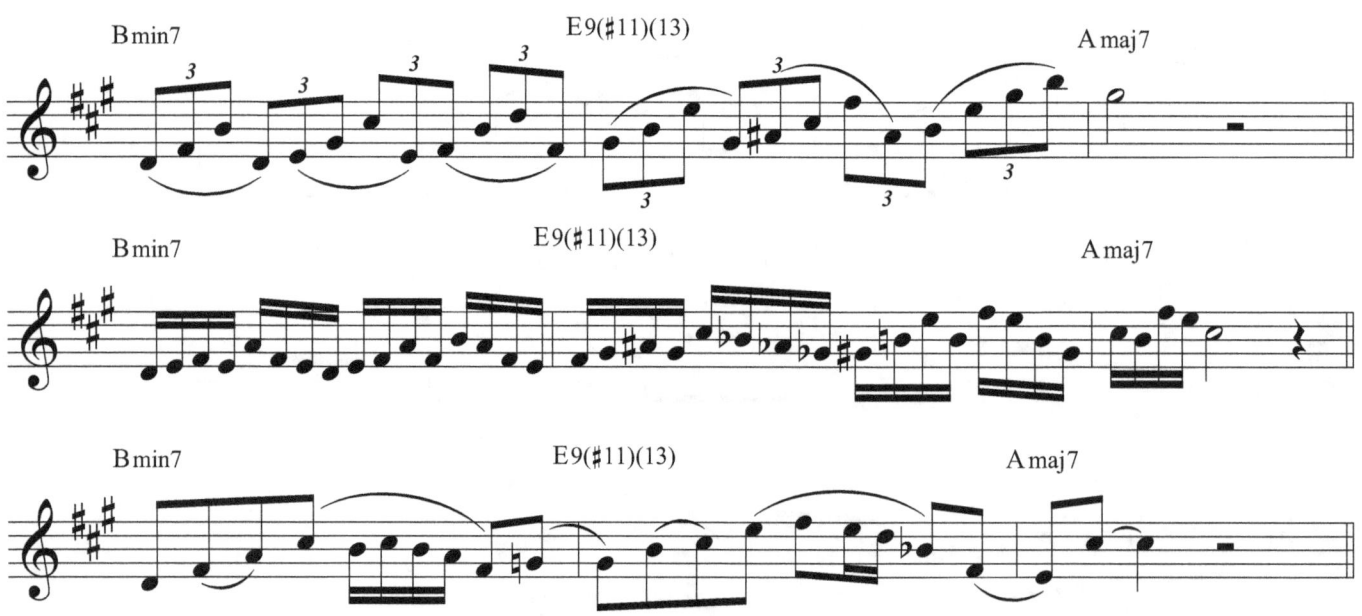

♭9-#11-♭13

#9-#11-♮13

#9-♭11-♭13

Altered

B♭ MAJOR

♮9 - ♮13 (Diatonic tensions)

♭9 - ♮13

#9-♭13

♮9-♭13

♭9-♭13

#9-♭13

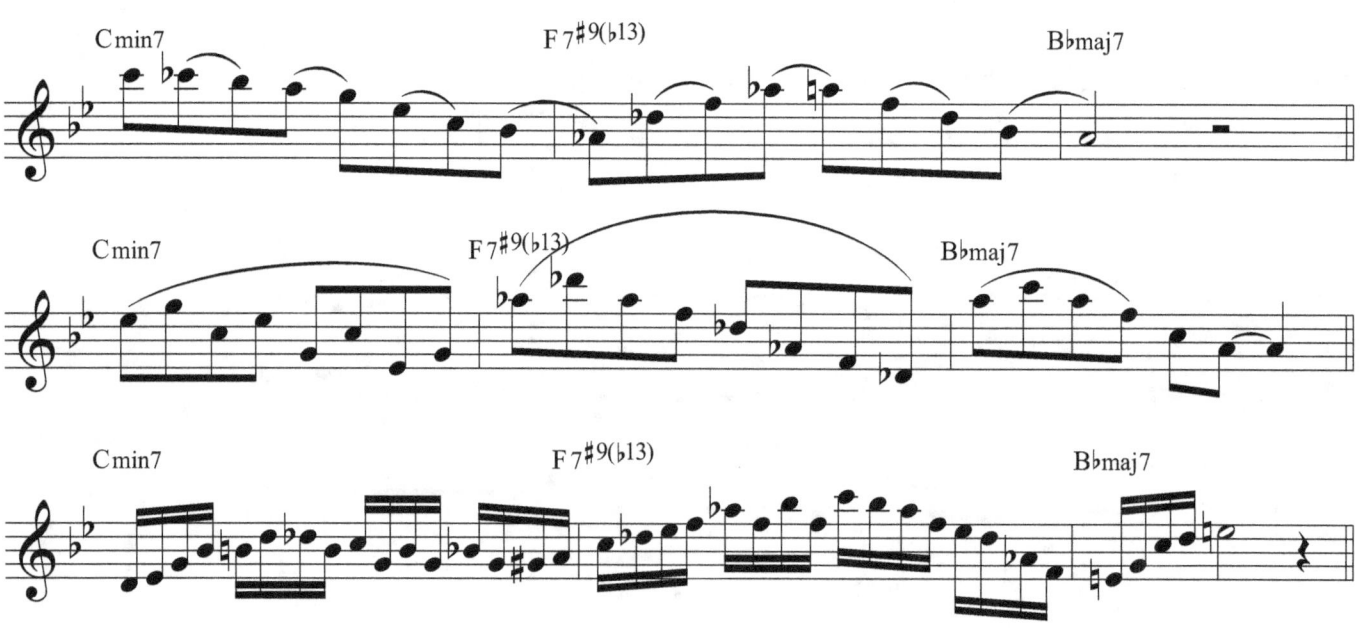

♮9-#11

♭9-#11

#9-#11

#11-♮13

#11 - ♭13

♭9 - #9 - ♮13

♭9-♯9-♭13

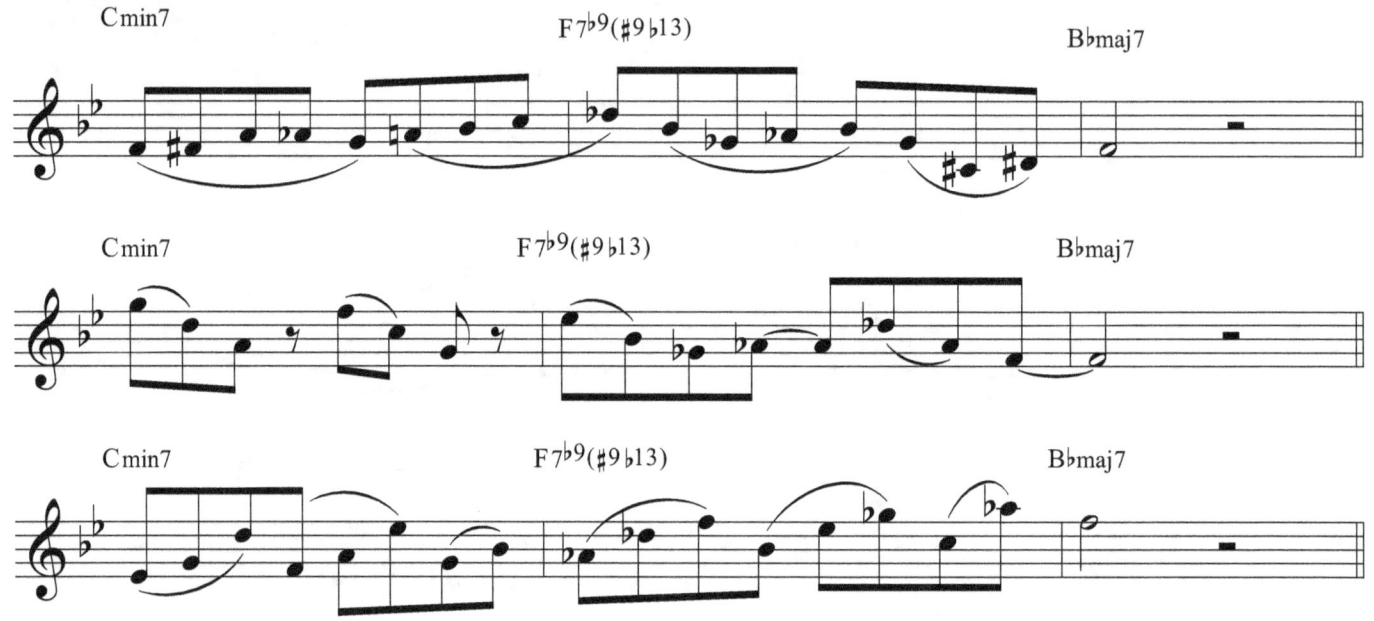

♭9-♯11-♭13

♮9 - #11 - ♭13

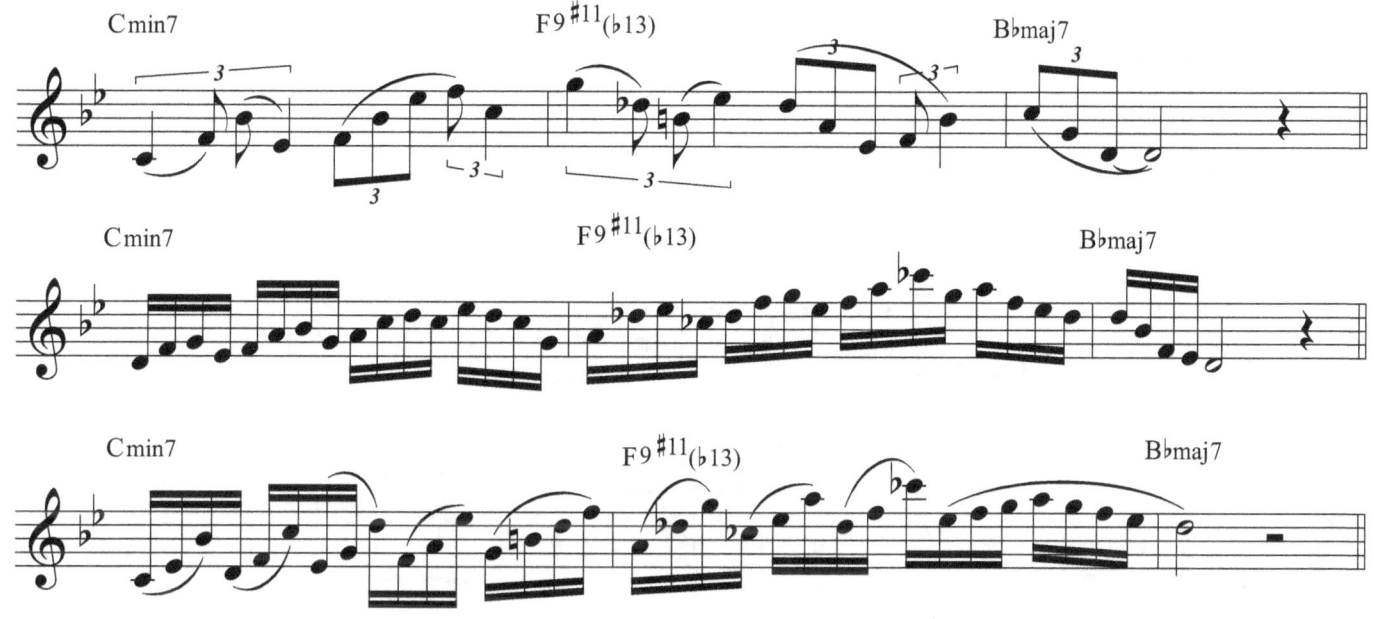

♮9 - #11 - ♮13

♭9-#11-♭13

#9-#11-♭13

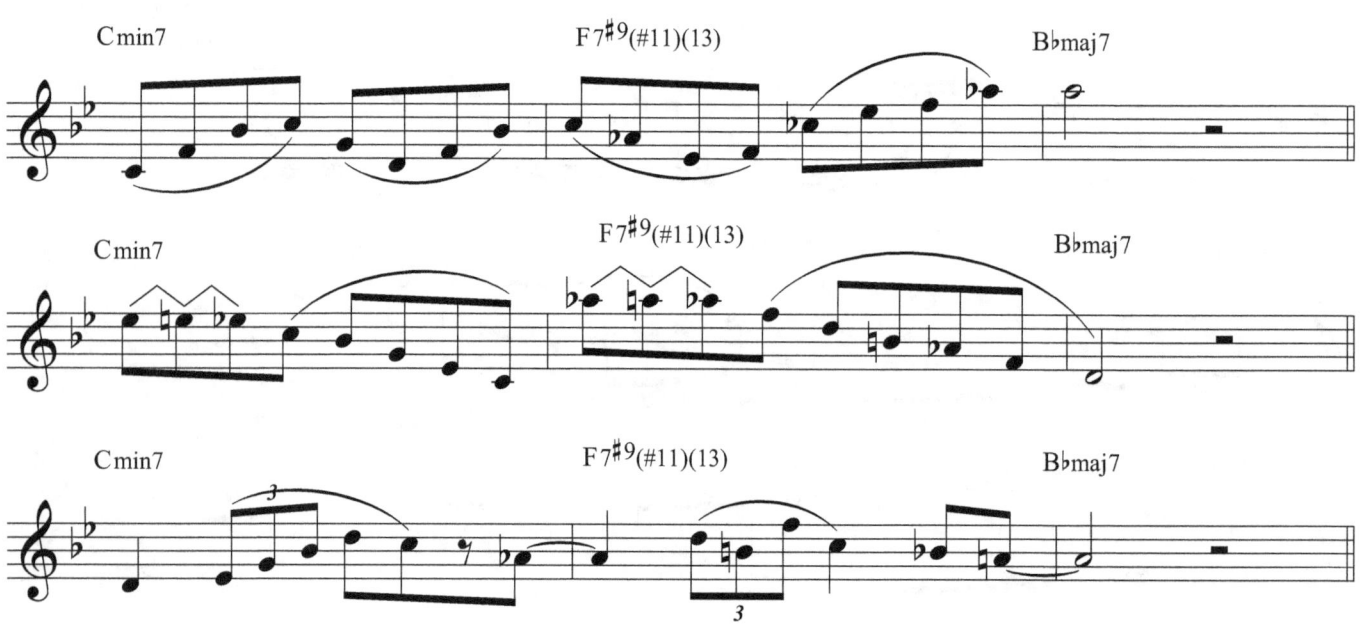

#9-♭11-♭13

Altered

B MAJOR

♮9 - ♮13 (Diatonic tensions)

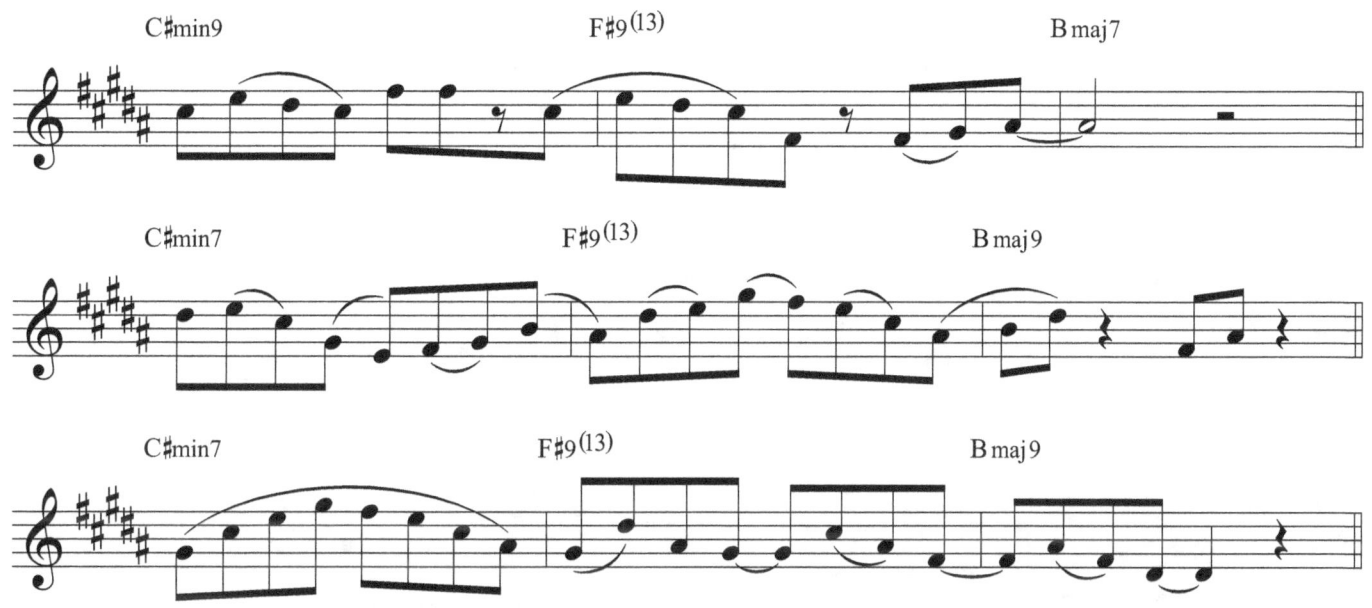

♭9 - ♮13

#9-♮13

♮9-♭13

♭9 - ♭13

♯9 - ♭13

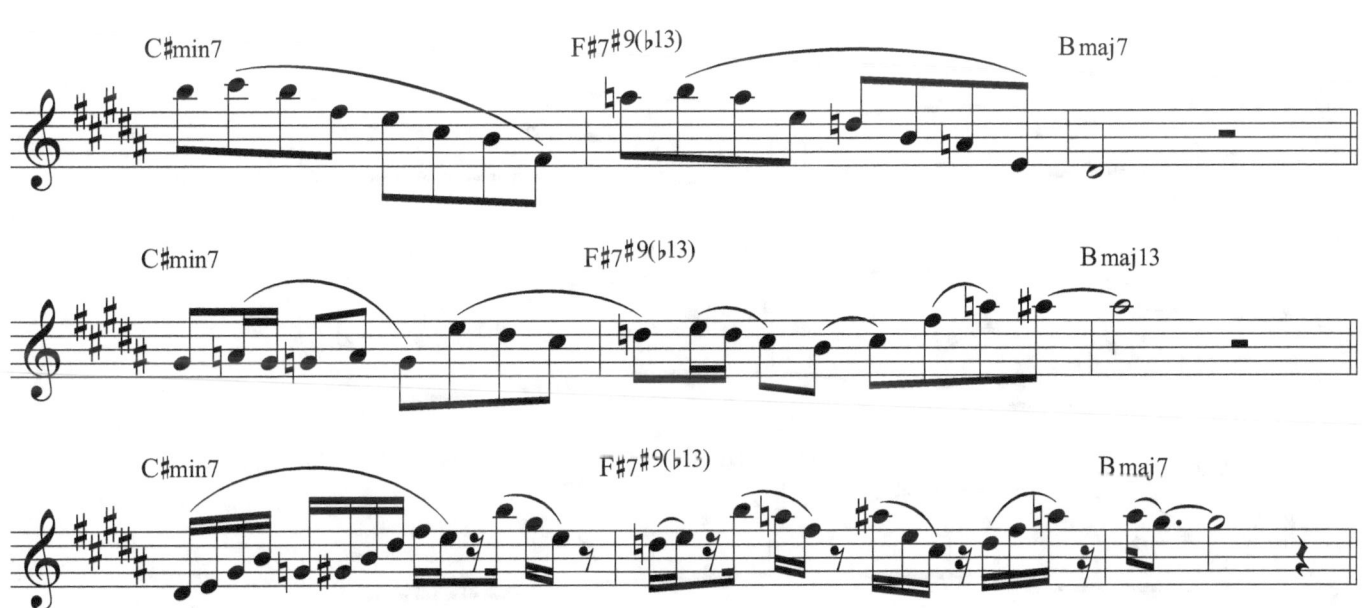

♮9-#11

♭9-#11

#9-#11

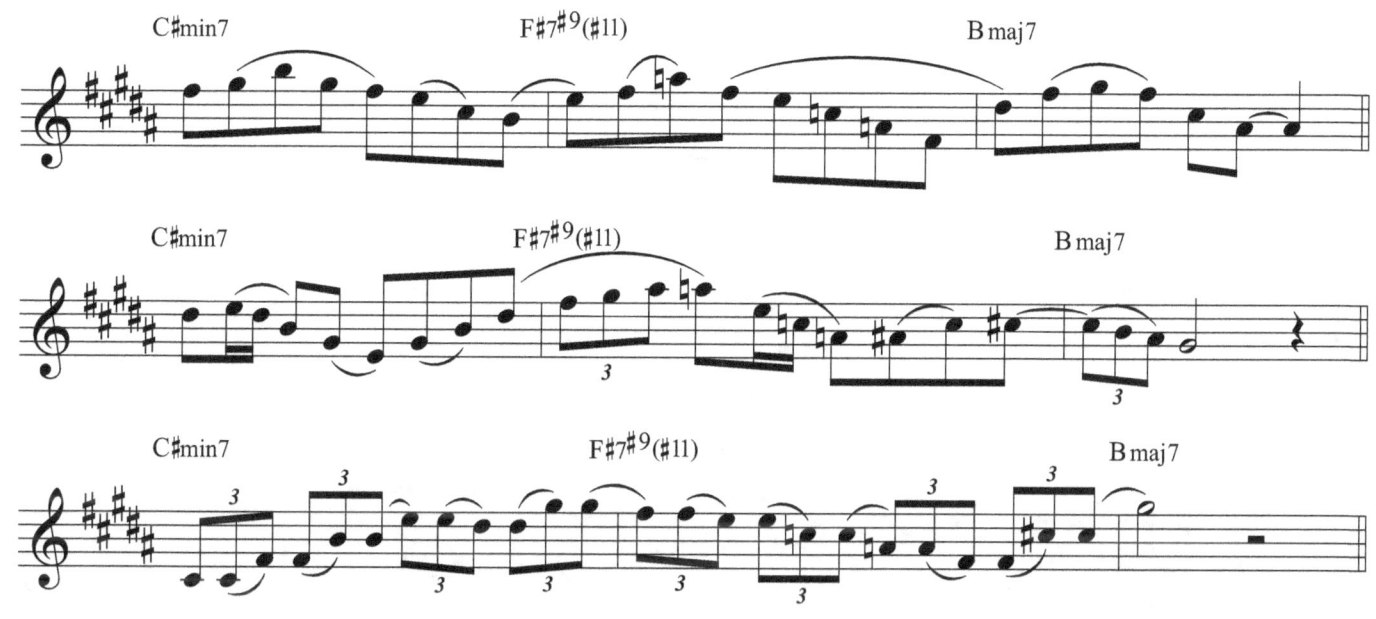

#11 - ♭13

♭9 - #9 - ♮13

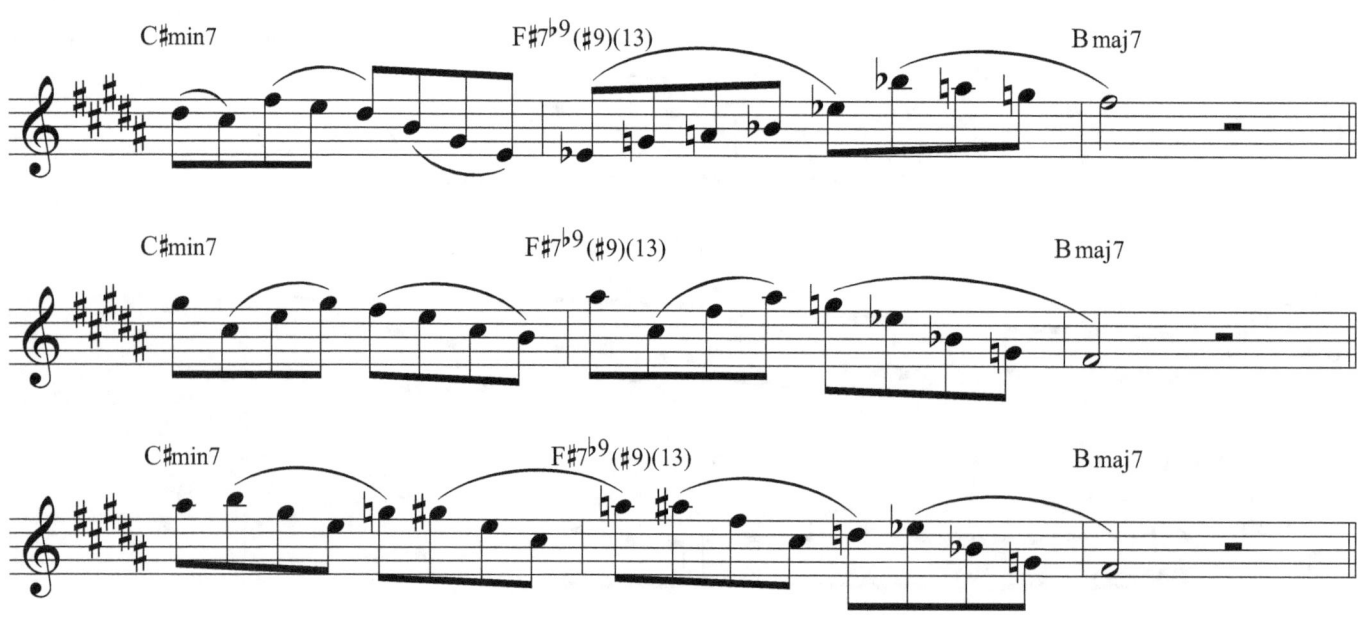

♭9-#9-♭13

♭9-#11-♮13

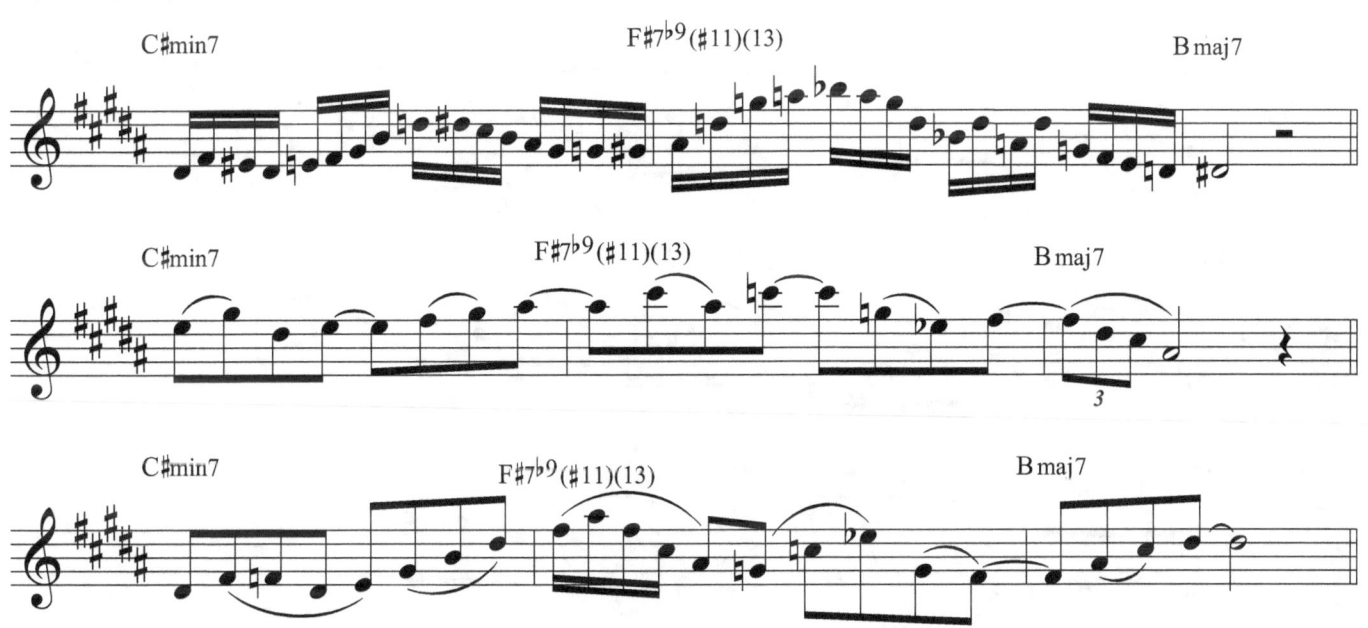

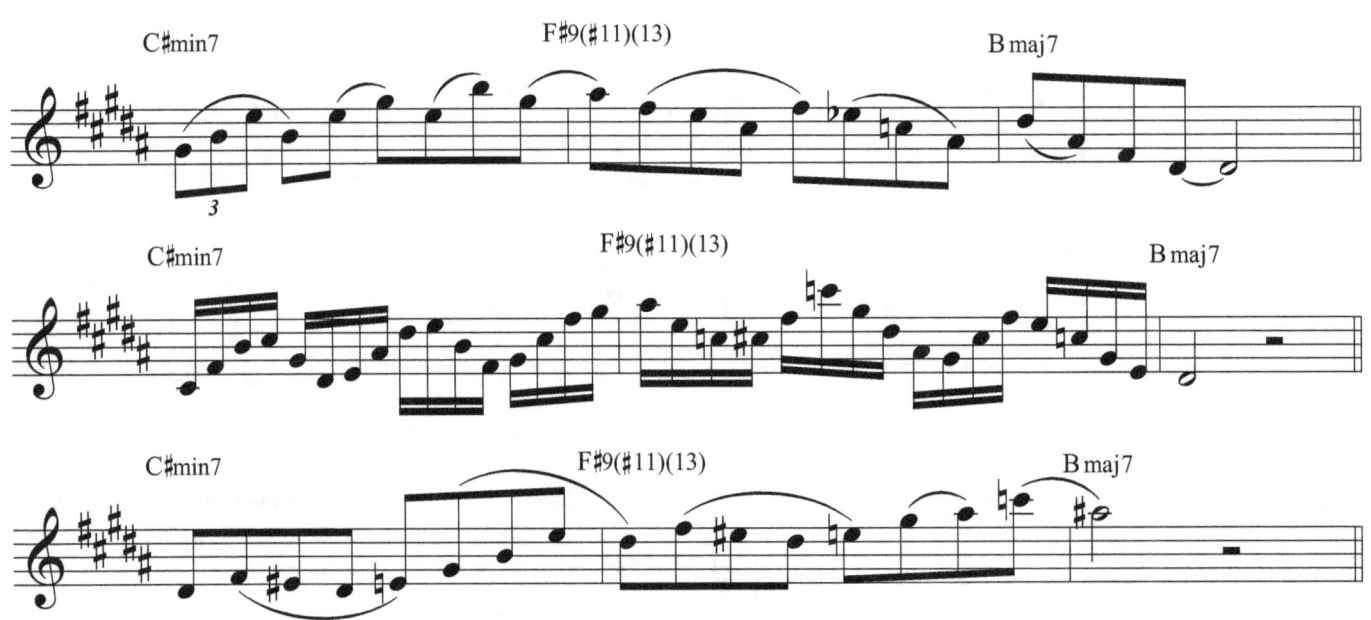

♭9-#11-♭13

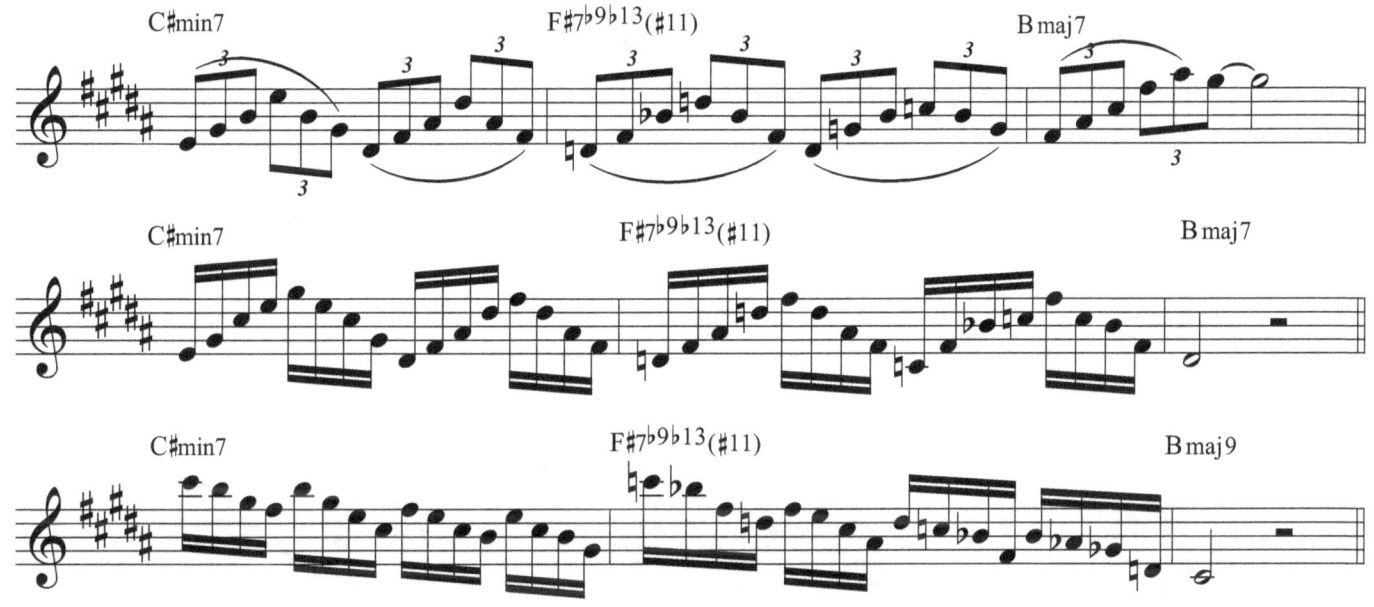

#9-#11-♮13

#9-♭11-♭13

Altered

BONUS JAZZ LICKS

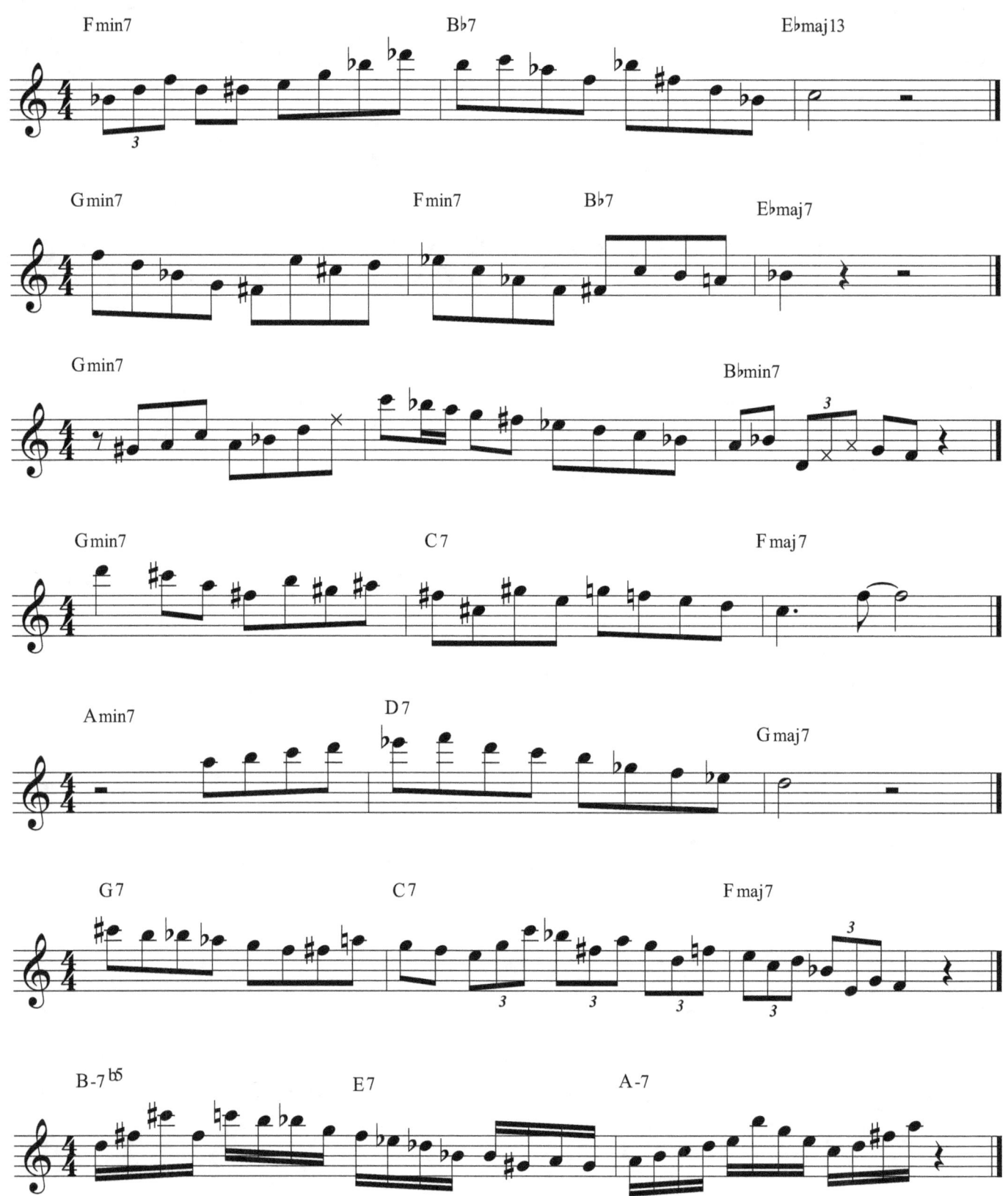

* If you only tap the accents in 7/4, you will be tapping in 4/4 time signature in 7/4

Other Books by Sarpay Özçağatay

UNLOCK Vol.I The Jazz Flute

UNLOCK Vol.II Technical Exercises

UNLOCK Vol.III Advanced Jazz Etudes

UNLOCK Vol.IV Intermediate Jazz Etudes

UNLOCK Vol.V Easy Jazz Etudes